SELF LOVE
JOURNAL FOR
WOMEN

Queendom

Copyright is reserved. Published in Cedartown GA by:

Dr. Darnetha Chester Publishing LLC dba Queendom 4145 Shackleford Rd. Norcross Georgia 30093

Tel: 678-501-5459

Email: darnetha@darnethaacademy.com Website: www.darnethachester.com

I hope readers will find this book to be an exceptional tool for becoming their best selves. If you could take a moment and leave me your feedback on Amazon, it would mean the world!

Thank you so much, Yours truly,

Dr. Darnetha Chester

About The Author

D r Darnetha was born and grew up in Atlanta and is a multi-talented author, coach, vocalist, and healer. Dr Darnetha's parents were both preachers, and she has a deep desire to inspire and motivate others via her profession. She holds several prestigious degrees and certifications from schools such as Beulah Heights Theological University, where she studied Leadership and Biblical Studies as an undergraduate, to American Inter-Continental University, where She gained a Master of Education in Instructional Technology with a concentration in Curriculum Design before going on to get a Doctorate in Transpersonal Counseling with an emphasis on Conscious Centered Living from The University of New York.

Dr Darnetha is a Psych K Facilitator and Life Coach who has helped people from various areas of life, from self-development to couples seeking to recover from infidelity. Dr Darnetha employs her knowledge, abilities, and experience in the healing process; she's multi-passionate and a trained soprano who graduated with a degree in Social Work from Atlanta Metropolitan College; she cares about humanity's well-being and prosperity.

She enjoys learning about spirituality and everything it includes. After many years as a school-teacher and raising her children, she chose to explore what would become one of my life's biggest hobbies — spirituality.

This desire prompted her to study everything that may aid personal development, including actively participating in spiritual ministry at my parents' church. This sparked an even stronger desire to learn more about spiritual growth.

Dr Darnetha has a beautiful team, including her mother Deloris, sister Davina, brother Eugene, and of course, God as her support system who help her navigate business and life. She is inspired by her three excellent young adult children, Jeremiah, Creasia, David, and a fantastic husband she married on Valentine's Day, 2021. She draws inspiration for her life and writing from the natural world and creatures surrounding her in Cedartown, Georgia.

Dr Darnetha is a self-described "naturalist" and wildlife enthusiast who enjoys spending time in the country and being surrounded by nature. She lives on a 2-acre plot of land with an organic fruit and vegetable garden that she enjoys and prepares delectable organic meals.

Since they married on Valentine's Day in 2021, her spouse has hugely supported her career ambitions! As a retired Aeronautical Mechanical Engineer, he helps out around the house when he can and spends his free time restoring old automobiles.

Dr Darnetha is a best-selling author of seven or more books, a curriculum designer for four online courses, and a life coach who uses her books, online courses, coaching practice, and speaking engagements to help individuals accomplish their personal and professional objectives. She draws on both her own and other people's experiences.

To instil in customers the belief that they have the power to make a positive difference in their life.

Her purpose is to use her personal experiences and those of the individuals she has worked with over the years to assist others in realizing their full potential. She has the skills and strategies to help individuals achieve through her books, online courses, and services, whether working through a specific issue or creating career-related objectives!

TABLE OF **CONTENTS**

WRITING SPACE

The blank space in this journal & workbook is for you take some time to reflect on your experiences and write down any final thoughts, feelings or participation in the exercises.

SECRET TO HAPPINESS

It's easy to comprehend how to live a happy life, but it's not always easy to realize. Here's a list of secrets that a lot of people are aware of but frequently overlook:

1. Before constructing a house, lay a solid foundation. Take the effort to develop your foundation, and you'll find that achieving your goals will be a lot easier.

2. Determine your level of spirituality and what it means to you.

3. Figure out how to bring more love into your life.

4. Rather than dwelling on the things you have yet to obtain, be glad for what you have today. Today is ideal—take use of it.

5. Be hands-on when selecting your fuel. The type of energy that propels your existence is entirely up to you.

6. Continue to educate yourself. Choose how often you want to learn and commit to doing so once a week. Learning is a form of evolution.

7. Make the most of your gifts by orienting your life around them in a way that will help you improve every day.

8. Recognize your vision and allow it to guide you toward your life's objectives and path

9. Invest time in expanding and learning your vocabulary. The key to success is communication. Speak up and know what you want to say.

10. Become as comfortable with chaos as you are with it.

11. Remember that honesty comes first, then necessities, and finally wants. Accomplish what you need to do now to do what you want later.

12. It's critical to solve difficulties in the past while perfecting the present to create the future you want. You will be rewarded if you do the right thing.

13. Get more than you need to live comfortably and disregard how much you believe you deserve.

14. Make time for planning by devoting 10% of your time to the other 90%. Your life is in your hands, even if it doesn't always feel that way.

15. Always use personal virtues to set goals. Ignore all of your "woulda, coulda, shoulda" desires and act while others merely dream.

16. Strive for financial independence, no matter how far away it appears. Every journey begins with a single step, no matter how long it takes.

17. Instead of changing a bad habit, learn to evolve. Many diets fail because going cold turkey is generally associated with failure.

18. Increase your boundaries to allow your heart and spirit to flow freely.

19. Instead of waiting, learn to take the initiative. Waiting on others might lead to a loss of productivity. Rather, forge your path.

20. Regardless of who began a problem, be the one to solve it.

21. Be a part of a community of like-minded people. Find people who can assist you and let them bring out the best in you.

SECRET TO HAPPINESS

EASY WAYS TO MAKE
YOURSELF SMILE

There are numerous compelling reasons to grin. SMILING MAKES YOU HAPPIER AND LOWERS

YOUR STRESS LEVELS. It can make you appear more approachable and appealing. According to some studies, it can even help you live longer by boosting your immune system.

You may sit and wait for something wonderful to happen that will make you happy. However, if you keep all of these benefits in mind, you can speed up the process. START WITH THESE EASY SUGGESTIONS FOR SMILING AT YOURSELF...

SMILE BECAUSE YOU ARE HAPPY. When you're feeling strong and fit, you're more likely to grin. Invest in your health and happiness. Allow yourself to be nurtured daily. TRY SOME OF THESE ACTIVITIES.

1. EAT HEALTHY FOODS.

Prepare nutrient-dense meals and snacks that are entirely made up of whole foods.

Eat a lot of fruits, vegetables, and whole grains. Sugar and salt should be used sparingly.

2. EXERCISE REGULARLY.

Continue to be active.

You'll want to persist with a range of workouts if you find a few that you enjoy.

3. GET A GOOD NIGHT'S SLEEP.

Make getting enough sleep a high priority.

Every night, I go to bed at about the same time. Maintain a dark and calm environment in your bedroom.

4. SPEND TIME IN THE GREAT OUTDOORS.

Green places have a way of uplifting our moods.

Visit a local beach or park for a picnic. In your backyard, hang a bird feeder.

Camping or mountain climbing are great ways to spend a weekend.

5. PAUSE TO LISTEN TO MUSIC

Make music that you can listen to while working out or doing domestic tasks.

Sing along to your favorite songs or branch out and try other genres.

6. GET A PASSION.

Flow, or the feeling of being involved and energized, is easier to achieve when you're doing something you enjoy.

Consider your childhood interests or go through periodicals for inspiration. Perhaps you'll enjoy painting landscapes or playing bocce ball.

TAKE A BREAK FROM TIME TO TIME.

Taking breaks during the day decreases stress and boosts productivity.

Take a break for a cup of tea or a stroll around the block.

SMILE BECAUSE YOU ARE SPREADING JOY.

Being generous can make you feel good on the inside and bring a big smile to your face.

Look for ways to share your good fortune.

WITH THESE ACTIVITIES, SPREAD SOME HAPPINESS...

1. PAUSE AND PAUSE AND PAUSE AND PAUSE AND PAUSE AND PAUSE AND PAUSE

A little thought can delight someone just as much as a costly present.

Demonstrate that you care about what others have to say.

Make eye contact with them and acknowledge their feelings.

2. OFFER YOUR SERVICES AS A VOLUNTEER.

Donate to worthwhile causes. Tutor high school students or walk dogs at a local shelter.

Volunteer Match and DoSomething are two organizations that can help you find volunteer opportunities.

3. ASSIST YOUR FRIENDS AND NEIGHBORS

Offer to assist handicapped or elderly neighbors with food shopping or yard labor.

Introduce yourself to new families and organize children's activities.

4. HOST A GET-TOGETHER

Extend your kindness. Make a monthly picnic or annual BBQ a tradition.

Make introductions between your pals.

5. DISTRIBUTE YOUR CREATIVE WORK.

Deliver baked goodies to a homeless shelter or the office.

If you prefer crafts to food, make photo frames or aromatic candles.

6. SEND A LETTER TO A FAMILY MEMBER OR FRIEND

When was the last time you received a letter written by hand?

Handwritten notes can make someone's day, especially for youngsters and elders.

7. BUY LOCAL

Many small businesses are struggling. Help them out by buying from neighborhood shops and restaurants whenever possible. Postpositive reviews online and tell your family and friends about your favorite finds.

8. CREATE A CIRCLE

Ask others to join you in your charitable endeavors.

A giving circle is a group of people who pool their money and other resources to support causes they care about.

OTHER THINGS TO DO TO MAKE YOU SMILE

1. MAKE SOME POPCORN AND WATCH A COMEDY MOVIE OR TELEVISION SHOW
2. VISIT A COMEDY LOUNGE.
3. AMUSE YOURSELF WITH A JOKE.
4. PLAY A SAFE AND FUNNY JOKE.
5. TEACH YOURSELF TO JUGGLE.
6. HAVE FUN WITH PUPPIES, KITTENS, AND OTHER PETS.
7. IN YOUR JOURNAL, WRITE 3 COOL THINGS THAT HAPPENED TODAY.
8. LEARN CARD OR MAGIC TRICKS AND SHOW OFF YOUR EXPERIENCE.
9. ENJOY A BACKWARDS DINNER, STARTING WITH DESSERT.
10. PLAY WITH YOUR CHILDREN AND ALLOW THEM TO SELECT THEIR ACTIVITY.
11. DEVOTE A PERSONAL DAY TO DOING WHATEVER YOU WISH.
12. TAKE A BREAK.
13. PLAY SOME MUSIC AND DANCE AS IF NO ONE IS EVEN LOOKIN.
14. READ A COMICAL BOOK.
15. PERFORM RANDOM KINDNESS ACTS.
16. REPEAT A SKILL YOU ENJOYED AS A CHILD, SUCH AS ROLLER-SKATING, ICE SKATING, OR SLEDDING.

7 STEPS TO SOLVE
ANY CHALLENGE

7 STEPS TO OVERCOME ANY OBJECTIVE

It has been suggested that life is nothing more than a never-ending sequence of issues to be addressed. The reality isn't nearly bleak, but life isn't without its difficulties. The obstacles you face and the answers you find will differ, but your approach to overcome them can be consistent.

You can reduce the psychological drama that obstacles can cause if you have a process in place!

Try this time-tested method:

1. KEEP A POSITIVE ATTITUDE.

When things don't go as planned, it's all too easy to get down on yourself. Negative thinking, unfortunately, makes you less capable. It can conceal the greatest solutions. Consider problems as puzzles to be solved, expecting that all will work out in the end.

2. CREATE THE PERFECT SOLUTION.

Aiming too low is a bad idea. It's customary to set a goal of simply surviving the challenge, but are you capable of going above and beyond? Can you think of a way to improve your circumstances even more than it was before? Make your difficulty a stepping stone to bigger and better things.

3. DISCUSS THE PROBLEM.

A major problem is frequently the result of a few little problems. Dealing with one tiny problem at a time will help you develop better control over your capacity to focus and prevent anxiety. You'll gain confidence and momentum as you continue to reduce the scope of the problem.

4. MAINTAIN YOUR FOCUS ON SOLUTIONS.

Don't be concerned about the future. Take your time to come up with the finest option. Look for a better answer once you've found a decent one. Continue looking until you're certain you can't find anything better. Keep in mind, too, that you need to give yourself adequate time to respond properly.

5. SEEK OUT ASSISTANCE.

Many folks are willing to assist. There's no reason to be embarrassed about seeking assistance. You'd gladly assist a friend or family member. They're also willing to assist you. Do not be afraid to ask.

6. BE READY FOR THE WORST-CASE SCENARIO.

What could go wrong with your plan? Have cures or preventative measures in place before deciding on a solution to counteract whatever might go wrong.

7. DEVOTE ALL OF YOUR ENERGY TO DEVELOPING YOUR SOLUTION.

Maintain your attention and carry out your strategy. Take note of how things are going and make any adjustments. Unless it's clear that you've picked an ineffective approach, never give up.

Use a defined process to solve problems and conquer hurdles in life.

Continue to take action until you've found a solution. Maintain an optimistic mindset and be inventive when brainstorming solutions. A challenge can often be used to your advantage.

FIND YOUR PURPOSE

AWAKEN YOUR TRUE CALLING

Introduction

There has been an unspoken rule that such people will succeed no matter how little effort they put in, while others will fail no matter how hard they try. The truth is that we all exist in an existential framework in which we are all given opportunities to achieve our life's Purpose. Despite the seemingly insurmountable barriers put against many people, few people have succeeded in achieving their objectives.

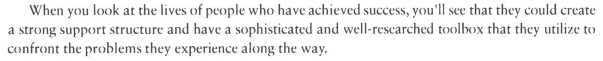

Surprisingly, many successful people may not necessarily originate from a privileged upbringing, but they all have one thing in common. They were able to seize the possibilities presented to them, and with strenuous effort, they could achieve success. They've discovered a way to live purposeful lives. When you look at the information on the website, you'll notice that.

When you look at the lives of people who have achieved success, you'll see that they could create a strong support structure and have a sophisticated and well-researched toolbox that they utilize to confront the problems they experience along the way.

Determined people do not achieve success by chance; rather, they have to analyze and troubleshoot before embarking on any undertakings or pursuing specific causes. When they encounter bottlenecks and face challenges, their toolkit contains many helpful tools, including resourceful people and mentors, skills to manage uncertainty and negativity, positive visualization techniques, goal-setting strategies, and alternative courses of action.

You can't afford to scroll through life without a clear awareness of your potential, aspirations, and personal qualities if you have this determination. You must set aside time to think about what makes you truly happy if you want to uncover and comprehend your mission. This becomes your road of passion, and once you've found it, you must follow it to the finish.

AWAKEN YOUR TRUE CALLING

CHAPTER 1: WHAT IS PURPOSE?

The Purpose is one of the driving motivations behind modern studies into personal development and social behavior. As more individuals become increasingly conscious of who they are, they feel compelled to learn more about their existence and the meaning of their lives. Knowing what purpose is and how it differs from goals is the best strategy to take when going into and discussing the topic of Purpose.

The Purpose is a cognitive process that helps you establish your life goals and gives you personal meaning. It is a central self-organizing objective that inspires goals, governs behavior, and provides you with the reality of existence.

Purpose guides the use of your finite personal resources, guiding your decisions and ambitions. Rather than dictating your actions, Purpose gives you direction, much like a compass does for a navigator. It is entirely voluntary to follow your mission, but there are considerable advantages.

Living following your Purpose allows you to be a self-sufficient force and an aggressive agent in pursuing and achieving your goals. As a result, the Purpose is crucial in assisting us in organizing our lives and developing tenacity that transcends time and context.

The Difference Between Purpose and Goals

Purpose and goals are not synonymous, although they are frequently referenced simultaneously in conversation and study.

The impact of goals on proximal behaviors is more precise. They are more focused on a certain endpoint and direct our behavior toward or away from it.

On the other hand, Purpose is a more general factor that drives behavior and motivates goals. Purpose motivates you rather than directing you toward a certain goal.

You must have a certain goal in mind. Unlike goals, which have definite outcomes, Purpose and values simply point you in the right direction.

Another way to think about Purpose is as a goal manager. Those who have a sense of purpose in their lives are better equipped to transition from one objective to the next and even handle many goals at once.

As a result, goals serve as a focal point and are generated and motivated by your life's purpose.

The Dimensions of Purpose

Purpose exists on a three-dimensional scale that includes strength, scope, and awareness. The scope of your mission is the extent to which it influences your life. A goal with a broad scope, for example, affects all of your behaviors, ideas, and emotions.

Compared to a purpose with a broad scope, a purpose with a narrow scope is more ordered but does not affect a wider range of actions.

In terms of Purpose, strength refers to the ability of the Purpose to impact your behaviors, thoughts, and emotions in domains relevant to its scope. A clear purpose greatly influences the actions that will help you achieve it. When combined with scope, strength determines how much your mission will affect your health, lifespan, and well-being.

A purpose that is marked by the immense power and a bigger reach, for example, will have a greater impact on your life. Furthermore, having a strong and broad purpose allows you to overcome hurdles and barriers that you may encounter on your trip.

The degree to which a person is knowledgeable and able to communicate their objective is measured by their awareness. Both scope and strength influence it. For a moment, consider the analogy of gravity. On Earth, gravity has a greater extent yet has a smaller impact.

We don't notice the gravitational forces that keep our feet firmly planted on the Earth while we go about our daily lives... If we were transported to Jupiter, which has twice as much gravitational attraction,

If we could raise our awareness of gravity's force, we would be far more conscious of it.

Purpose-driven behaviors can be engaged to motivate people to take action. It takes less work to follow a cause when you are aware of it than if you are utterly clueless.

The Pursuit of Multiple Purposes

It's not rare for people to have many life objectives. On the other hand, having several purposes can only be advantageous up to a point, after which such purposes merely serve to diminish resource allocation.

For example, if you are pursuing a single goal, you may grow disheartened if the hurdles and barriers you confront seem too great to overcome. When you have many purposes that are independent of one another, on the other hand, you will immediately shift your attention and focus to the other when you encounter a hindrance or challenge in one.

This movement between life goals might help you live a more purposeful life and improve your chances of getting good results.

On the other hand, multiple aims may cause you to switch from one to the next frequently, obstructing your progress. For a smart and long-term strategy, you'll need a manageable number of life goals to which you can devote sufficient resources and effort to reap tangible results.

Critical Elements of Purpose

Some factors are required for you to have a purposeful life. You must be constant in your actions. This will serve as a driving force to help you overcome hurdles, stay focused, and explore alternate solutions regardless of changing environmental conditions. People who live a meaningful life are more consistent in their public and private lives in their actions.

You must also be mentally adaptable. This means that your mission allows you to be more flexible in the face of shifting demands, difficulties, and opportunities. Adaptability in the face of adversity

When you manage your environment, both psychologically and physically, you will have fewer issues than individuals who live aimlessly.

Finally, having a purpose allows you to effectively manage your resources, such as time and energy, to achieve your goals. Any other useless actions or behaviors are avoided, and the resources they would have used are redirected to the purposeful ones.

These components might also be considered as required ingredients for living a meaningful life. It's nearly hard to discover and achieve your life's mission without them.

CHAPTER 2: KEYS TO FINDING YOUR PASSION

Most people try to blame their failures and uncertainties on a lack of passion for one or more things. As a result, they're stuck in an endless cycle of pursuing dull and uninteresting activities.

Contrary to popular assumptions, finding your passion is not as difficult as it may appear. Passion isn't a rare commodity saved only for a select few. Rather, it is a gift that has been given to everyone. The first and only thing we need is the right mindset to discover our true calling. Work is intended to be enjoyable, so take the time to figure out what you enjoy doing.

Rather than seeing yourself as hopeless because you haven't found your calling, imagine yourself surrounded by limitless opportunities. The truth is that your imagination is the only thing stopping you from doing what you love. Some straightforward keys will lead you to uncover your purpose and meaning in life, allowing you to break free from this prison of ambiguity and lack of passion.

Give yourself the chance to succeed.

Despite its enormous importance, allowing oneself to be passionate is sometimes overlooked as a minor and insignificant stage in discovering your passion. It's possible that you're not following your passion because you don't believe you deserve to be passionate about it.

On the other hand, everyone has the right to feel enthusiastic about their goals in life. When you wake up, you have every right to be excited about your life. If you allow yourself to follow your passions, you will be better positioned to serve others.

You must alter your mental image if you want to connect with, accept, and appreciate what you do. Once you can link your identity to your passion, it will be much easier for you to find fulfillment in the things you do in life.

Allow Yourself to Explore

There exists one true passion for every one of us, and everything else is not worth the effort and focus. This creates the all-or-nothing mindset. Unfortunately, the danger with this perspective is that it makes you miss other opportunities in your pursuit to live passionately.

You have to understand that there is a spectrum of possibilities between your fulfillment and enjoyment in what you do. At one end of the spectrum is the work you hate and can't do under every circumstance. The task you truly enjoy, which thrills and energizes you just thinking about it, is on the other end of the spectrum.

Between these two points is a huge range of possibilities for work that bores you, work that makes you feel indifferent, work those challenges and stimulates you, and tasks that make you come alive with excitement.

The best thing you can do is move toward the direction on the spectrum that makes you come alive. As you pursue what you love, you will come across options to lead you to your ultimate life's purpose. The more aggressive and passionately you seek that work that excites you, the more efficient you will

Become at filtering out everything else that tends to drain your energy and distract you from your desired outcome.

It's crucial to remember that you'll have to become used to liking work before you can love it. Do not, however, waste enough of your time and energy hating work because it can blind you, deplete you, and lead you to lose sight of your passion.

Look Closely at What You're Doing

The opportunities to do what we love are right in front of us. Unfortunately, we tend to think that we can't make a meaningful living out of what we do. When you can change your perspective, you might find the things that you've been looking down on are the most fascinating.

Question Yourself

In an attempt to figure out what they are passionate about, most people fail to ask themselves the powerful questions. You need to give yourself time and let go of other activities to engage with your passion.

Often, we let other things take precedence at the expense of exploring the things that excite us. To succeed in finding your passion, you need to set aside quality time to figure out what makes you excited. Some of the questions that you need to ask yourself that can lead you to discover your purpose and passion are:

- What would you do, even if you won't get paid for it?
- Do you have any gifts or skills that you can share with the world?
- When in your life did you feel most creative?
- What comes naturally to you?
- What have you accomplished in the past that was successful?

Asking yourself these questions will awaken your subconscious mind and allow you to start searching within yourself to discover your passion.

Always Test Your Passion

Before you take yourself down a certain path and incur expenses, you need to test your passion for establishing its credibility. You can accomplish this by taking courses online or at your local college to determine if you have a true passion for the area you want to specialize in. Going through this process of testing your

Passion will inform you whether it is real or just a fleeting fantasy with no possibility for long-term fulfillment.

After you've found your passion, start living it the right way. It will pay for you to immerse yourself in a passionate and deliberate action rather than dipping your toe in forever.

CHAPTER 3: BEING PROACTIVE

As an individual, you are solely responsible for your own life. Your behaviors result from all of your choices, not the circumstances. Only you have the power and responsibility to transform your life and make things happen.

Proactive people are aware of their Purpose, and they understand that it is their behavior, not the situations or events around them, that keeps them from realizing their actual calling in life.

Your actions directly result from the conscious decisions you make based on your value systems. We are all proactive beings by nature, and if the events around us shape our lives, it is because we have actively chosen to allow those circumstances to govern us.

Reactive is the polar opposite of proactive. When you are reactive, the physical environment has a greater impact than your value system. When the weather is nice around a reactive person, for example, everything else is fine, and their attitude and performance are unaffected. If the weather changes, their position and performance will also alter.

People that take action are in charge of their future and goals. It makes little difference whether it rains or not for proactive people. They will continue to generate high-quality work because their value systems motivate them.

If you wish to live a purposeful life, you must reduce your desires to a value that is important to your existence. Even though external stimuli occasionally influence you, your response to these impulses should be value-based. You must own up to and admit that the decisions you've made thus far in your life have shaped you into the person you are now to stay on track in achieving your objectives and life's Purpose.

Taking Initiative

Our core nature is set up to act rather than be acted upon. In the end, we can choose how we react to the situations we find ourselves in. Embracing the leadership has nothing to do about being aggressive, arrogant, or pushy; it has everything to do with being resourceful.

Everything depends on our willingness to take personal responsibility for our actions. Too many people are content to wait for something to happen or for someone else to take care of their business.

You must be proactive and produce unique solutions to the difficulties you or your organization encounter if you want to get a decent job that revolves around your passion and one you will love for a long time. You must take charge of the situation and do whatever it takes to complete the task.

Prevail or Be Prevailed Upon

There is a significant distinction between those who take the initiative and those who do not. Life is just in the sense that everyone can direct their lives toward their goals. On the other hand, those around you will use you to achieve their own goals if you don't take advantage of the opportunity in front of you. By combining your creativity and resourcefulness, you may establish a proactive culture in your life, regardless of your personality. There are no longer any justifications for being at the mercy of the environment. Instead, you may take charge of

Become More Aware of Your Proactivity

Analyzing where you put your resources is a terrific method to become more conscious of your level of proactivity. Each of us has a variety of issues in our daily lives. You might make a circle of concern and try to isolate the things we have no emotional or mental engagement with.

When you begin to explore the issues in your circle of concern, it will become evident that there are certain things over which you have no influence and others over which you may have some power. You can reorganize the things you discover you have power over into a smaller circle of influence.

When you've figured out how to allocate your time and energy, The amount of your proactivity can then be determined by comparing the circle of concern and the sphere of influence. Those who are proactive in their lives are concerned about their life's Purpose and concentrate their efforts on matters within their sphere of influence.

They only pay attention to the things over which they have control. On the other hand, Reactive persons get far more immersed in the circle of worry. They are more concerned with other people's flaws, environmental issues, and conditions beyond their control. This leads to a perplexed and aimless life marked by blaming and accusing attitudes, reactive language, and increasing victimization.

You will not achieve anything as long as you operate within the circle of care and focus on the items within that circle. Nonetheless, if you can shift your focus and start working in your sphere of influence, you will generate positive energy that will change you and your actions.

It's encouraging to understand that the way you respond to situations can significantly impact your whole status. You can vary the nature of the findings by changing a portion of your chemical formula. If you want to change your situation and find your life's purpose, you should focus on the things you can influence.

CHAPTER 4: BEGIN WITH THE END IN MIND

None of us are invincible. We will all depart this planet at some point, and whether you've fulfilled your Purpose or not, your time will be up with no chance of a bonus. Keeping the end in mind will assist you in aligning your life with your Purpose. You must live your life in such a way that everyone will praise your efforts, accomplishments, and character. Having this outlook on life can help you better grasp your Purpose and how to go about achieving it.

Living With the End in Mind

What does it mean to spend your life to reach your destination in mind? It states that you have a picture, an image, or a paradigm of the end as a picture, image, or paradigm of the end as a picture, image, or paradigm of the end as a picture, image, o

Everything in life is viewed through the lens of this point of reference. Every aspect of your life may be seen in context with the rest of your life and what matters to you. By keeping the end in mind, you can be certain that whatever you do on any given day will not alter your overall Purpose in any way.

Your life, like a pilot's voyage, should begin with a destination in mind. This implies you should have a clear idea of where you want to go to better grasp where you are now and the measures you'll need to take to get there.

People frequently find themselves achieving empty achievements. They understand that their achievement came at the cost of something considerably more precious and significant. People of all professions and areas of life strive for a higher salary, greater recognition, or a specific level of professional skill. However, they may not recognize that their desire to reach these lofty ambitions can cause them to lose sight of the most important things, and they may not realize this until it is too late. When you examine what you want to be remembered for at the end of your life, your genuine definition of success will emerge.

Design or Default

Suppose you can't build a sense of self-awareness and take responsibility for your mental creations in your life. In that case, you're encouraging individuals outside your circle of influence to mold your life by default.

Stop living the scripts offered to you by your family, associates, and other people's agendas if you want to awaken your true calling.

These scripts are based on people rather than principles, and they will not bring you to your Purpose.

Writing Your Script

Since we already have a lot of scripts handed over to us, writing our scripts can be seen more as a re-scripting process.

In developing your self-awareness, you can discover some ineffective scripts deeply embedded in you that are completely incongruent with your values.

You are responsible for writing new, more effective scripts with your deepest values and principles.

Develop a Personal Mission Statement

The most effective way to integrate the end into your journey is to develop a personal mission statement. Your mission statement should focus on what you want to be, what you want to do, and the values upon which your character and achievements are found.

To write a meaningful personal statement, you have to start at the center of your circle of influence. The center consists of the lens through which you view the world. It enables you to deal with your values and visions and helps you mentally create the life you were meant to live.

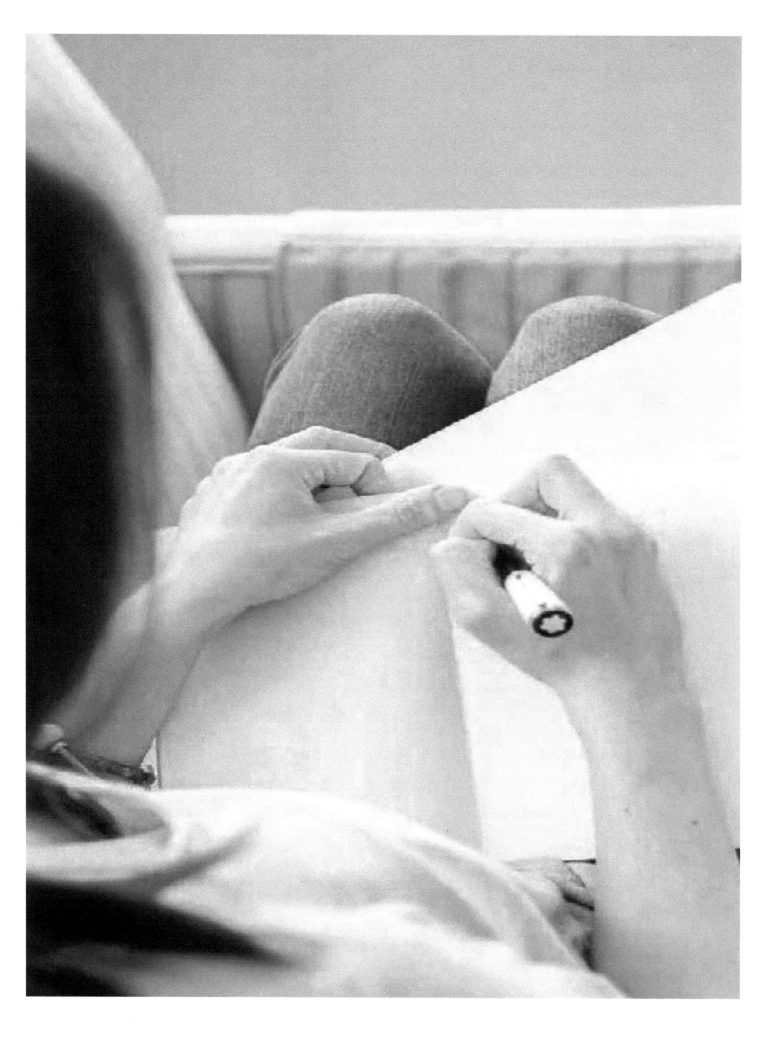

CHAPTER 5: LEVERAGING POSITIVE VISUALIZATION

To achieve your objectives and complete your responsibilities, you must use creative visualization. Our brains cannot distinguish between the real, and the imagined when it comes to our internal mental fabrication. The mental images you produce have a real and palpable influence on your body. You may achieve your goals and live a worthwhile life by placing your own belief in the process of imagining.

Building a Foundation

Like any other physical or mental function, visualization requires a solid foundation on which to build. You must comprehend

The greatest sensory qualities, whether visual or audio, that your mind experiences.

Bring to recollect the ideas that ran through your head before previous failed or successful experiences. You'll realize that your thought pattern caused you to act in a certain way, which attracted the events and circumstances you desired. This demonstrates how visualization and images may help you make significant changes in your life.

Creative Visualization

A creative visualization is a mental approach that employs the mind's and imagination's ability to help you create changes in your life and get closer to your Purpose. You can use creative imagination to mold your personality, surroundings, and habits and attract the opportunities and things you want in life.

Repeated ideas will affect your subconscious mind and cause events to occur. Your wants, habits, reactions, and behaviors are all controlled by your subconscious. They are likewise drawn to similar situations. Through creative visualization, your mind will build mental scenarios of specific events and incidents in your life.

The more you give the fuel to your thoughts, the more powerful they become. The most significant and powerful instrument for creative vision is your imagination. We create the automobiles, computers, and buildings that you see today through creativity.

Integrating Creative Visualization into Your Life

You must include vision in your life if you want to live a purposeful, focused existence. Like learning to drive a car or play a musical instrument, visualization will take time and effort. If you want to get the full benefits of visualization, you must be disciplined, devote time, and practice until you master the technique.

The length of time it takes for you to see results is entirely dependent on your imagination's vividness as well as your level of dedication. Experts recommend practicing for 15 to 20 minutes each day. You can lower the time to only a few minutes every day to perfect the skill and grow more comfortable with the technique.

According to research, visualization works best when used with a relaxing technique. According to the study, while your body is calm, your mind is equally relaxed and not under conscious control, allowing you to daydream.

Many visualizations and imaging techniques can be utilized to conjure up the desired feeling and provide you with a sense of purpose. Guided visualization is one of the most popular techniques. It entails seeing yourself obtaining a goal and then visualizing yourself going through the process of achieving that objective.

Creative visualization can help you overcome the practical challenges to achieving your Purpose by combining your thoughts with mental images and emotions to produce actions and results. You will train your subconscious mind to make the image a reality by repeating the same thoughts every day.

CHAPTER 6: MASTERING PERSONAL MANAGEMENT

An important process in purposeful living is personal management. Personal management helps direct and establish you on the right path toward your destiny. Its simplest definition, personal management, refers to the planning, organizing, directing, and coordinating various aspects of your life to achieve your life's Purpose.

To effectively manage yourself, you need to possess a strong and independent will. Personal management is a necessary skill in today's complex world to recognize our hidden potential. We need to Master effective personal management principles if we're going to maximize the usage of our skills to come up with solutions to our daily challenges.

Personal management helps you control your life and build meaningful interpersonal relationships to pursue your Passion and Purpose. You can break from your confines and live a fulfilled life through personal management.

The Four Rules of Self-Management

If you want to become an effective person who knows how to manage your affairs and take control of your life, there are four rules that you need to observe. These rules will act as your guiding system as you work toward discovering your Purpose.

The first thing that you must do is map your life. This step will allow you to understand who you are, where you are coming from, and where you are going. This will provide you with an orientation of Purpose and direction. Mapping out your life is the core of every success that you will achieve in your life.

The second rule that you need to observe is to review your assumptions. Everyone has a belief system and a unique perspective to assess ourselves. Some of the assumptions that you hold can hinder your journey to achieving your life goals and finding happiness. Reviewing the assumptions that you hold will allow you to look inside yourself and count your weaknesses and strengths.

Once you've reviewed your assumptions, the third rule you need to observe is to organize yourself and your potential to achieve your desired goals. Without this self-organization, even the skills you possess can be easily dissolved and rendered useless.

The fourth rule is to develop your abilities closely linked with self-organization. This includes the development and improvement of your imagination, introspection, and willpower, along with other skills. These will greatly enhance your capacity to express yourself.

Power of a Strong and Independent Will

Will refers to making decisions and choices and acting following them. It is a proactive approach to carrying out the program that you have developed for your life. The extent of Your integrity measures the degree of will development in your life.

The higher your integrity level, the more independent you will be. Integrity is simply your ability to make commitments and follow through with them.

Effective personal management requires that you prioritize things in your life. As a self-manager, your discipline to organize the various aspects of your life should come from within. You must be a discipline of your value system.

Being independent will give you the power to do something even when you don't want to, as long as it aligns with your underlying values.

To develop your will, you must start by setting up and achieving small resolutions. This can give you the momentum and the zeal to move on and take on more substantial assignments.

You can boost your willpower through clarity of Purpose, the priority of Purpose, good planning, and determination.

Time Management

Another essential personal management skill is your ability to manage your time.

Time management skills help you organize and execute your tasks based on your priorities. Each of us has the same number of hours and how we use them determines the extent of our success or failure

To manage your time, you need to prioritize and discipline yourself. Whenever tasks overwhelm you, you should learn to delegate effectively to reliable and capable people.

CHAPTER 7: LEARNING TO OVERCOME NEGATIVITY

Resilience is defined as the ability to persevere in the face of adversity while maintaining hope, mental health, and healthy coping mechanisms. Resilient people can stay focused and come out stronger after going through adversity.

As you move closer to your Purpose, you will encounter many problems that will demand you to have self- confidence and new coping abilities to get through them.

Any negative element that tries to throw you off course can be conquered with resilience.

Resilient people usually have particular personality traits that influence how they approach and overcome difficulties. Some of the following personality traits have an impact on resilience.

Optimism

Optimism is when you feel that things will improve and that the current difficulties and challenges you face will be overcome.

Independence

Self-determination relates to the ability to make life decisions and plan your actions without relying on others to do so for you.

Control and Responsibility

This implies a sense of calm and inner peace that comes from believing that you can make a difference in the bad situations that you may encounter from time to time.

To overcome negativity, you must learn how to train yourself to think positively, even when you are in a difficult and stressful circumstance. Even when everything appears to be going wrong, you have the intrinsic ability to turn your negative ideas into more positive ones and find humor in situations.

While your prior experiences may have been negative, and your current circumstance isn't ideal, this does not guarantee that your future possibilities will be compromised unless you allow them to. Your life's Purpose may not be on a straight route paved with cupcakes and rainbows, which is why you must intentionally push away the difficult moments and focus on the end objective.

How to Develop Personal Resilience

You must take purposeful actions to improve your resilience levels to face problems in your life. The first step is to start incorporating positive affirmations into your everyday routine. Words have tremendous power.

Whatever you say has a chance of becoming a reality. When you talk favorably about your life, you'll be surprised at how quickly things improve.

Life does not always provide you with simple solutions. You must work for it and make it a goal, regardless of the circumstances. When you can raise your drive to overcome all odds, you will build your resilience reservoirs.

You will express yourself better if you can learn how to build cultural bridges and improve your communication abilities.

When confronted with a challenging situation, know yourself better and seek the assistance you require. When it comes to some of the obstacles you'll face, you'll need someone to listen to you and someone to lean on. When you have improved communication, it will be easier to seek guidance when confronting a problem related to your Purpose.

Making decisions is a necessary part of your daily routine. When confronted with obstacles and problems, your ability to approach them with an open mind can assist you in overcoming them, regardless of how challenging they are. These abilities will aid you in navigating and maintaining your focus on your ultimate goals and life's purpose.

The Brain and Resilience

Modern science helps us learn about the biological processes of the brain and how it affects our reasoning, determination, and ability to pull through difficult situations. Some brain parts produce chemicals that boost our happiness levels, while others bring about anxiety and fear.

To be mentally, physically, and behaviorally healthy, we need to change our perspectives and thought patterns even in stressful situations. You can awaken your potential to stand firm and display resilience even in difficult times by speaking to your subconscious. By thinking positively about what you are currently

By doing, you will find satisfaction, happiness, and a reason to continue moving forward.

CHAPTER 8: LEARNING TO LIVE A BALANCED LIFE

Four dimensions can describe a healthy and balanced life. These are mental, physical, spiritual, and social. By exercising all four aspects regularly, you will improve your life and general outlook toward work and your Purpose. However, this will require time and proactivity.

An investment in yourself is the single most powerful investment you can make in finding your Purpose. You are the instrument of your performance, and if you want to be successful, you must understand the value of exercising and sharpening your life.

The Physical Dimension

This dimension involves ensuring that you are taking care of your physical body by eating right, exercising, relaxing, and getting enough rest. Exercise is an extremely important activity. While it isn't urgent, most people wish they didn't have to do it and give it a low priority. For many, we simply believe that we don't have enough time to exercise, which is itself a distorted paradigm. Exercising for a minimum of 30 minutes a day is not much if you consider the numerous benefits that you will gain from physical activity.

Spiritual Dimension

We are spiritual beings that incline a higher being. The spiritual dimension forms the core and the center of your commitment to your value system. It is a private and vital area of your life. It draws upon the resources that uplift and inspire you toward awakening your Purpose.

Mediation is one of the spiritual dimension's most basic exercises. It aids in the strengthening, renewing, reaffirming, and centering of your commitment to serve. These are the exact things you'll need to live your life's purpose. Nature has a way of endowing people who immerse themselves in it with its special blessings.

The Mental Dimension

Formal education provides you with discipline and mental development. However, the moment you leave this external discipline of the school, many tend to let our minds sink into atrophy. We tend to avoid engaging in serious reading, and the passion for exploring new subjects dies away. We no longer think analytically, and we don't write as creatively as we used to.

Continuing education is important because it hones and expands our minds. To be a proactive and purposeful individual, you need to find as many ways to educate yourself and train your mind as possible. Reading good literature will give you access to the best minds of authors and philosophers.

You can set a goal to read one book a month and increase it as you learn to read faster. Remember, a person who doesn't read is no better off than someone who can't read.

The Social Dimension

The social dimension focuses on interpersonal relationships, creative cooperation, and empathic communication with those around you. Since your emotional and social life is manifested through your relationships with others, they are often tied together. Renewing our social dimension doesn't take as much time as the other, and it can be done daily through our interactions with others.

The true joy in life comes from being used for a purpose you are aware of. Aim to be completely used up by the time you come to the end of your time.

Conclusion

In your quest to awaken your true calling, you need to focus on the fundamental components that motivate you. This will allow you to avoid wasting time on something not in sync with your potential. It is disastrous to spend time chasing after the wrong goals, whether in your personal life, career, or business. Instead, you need to find quality time and ask yourself some soul-searching questions.

Find out whether you are currently happy in your life and think about what you can do to improve it. Start to take care of unfinished business and find things you are passionate about. Reflect on your life as much as possible and continue to recalibrate things when needed. It isn't a must for you to reach

Adulthood before you can discover your life's purpose. LePurposetake the time to think about your choices whenever you can.

You must find what you are passionate about because focusing your time and energy on the wrong thing can cause you to become unmotivated and disappointed with your life. And remember that sometimes the light you need to shine on your path is right inside you.

BELIEVE IN YOUR VISION

Introduction

Hello and welcome to our brief introduction to the law of attraction's power, and more significantly... How to use the law of attraction in your daily life!

The New Thought Movement's Law of Attraction proposes that you may attract extraordinary or wrong situations to yourself simply by changing your perspective.

Right things will come your way if you stay cheerful, and your overall happiness will improve. If you allow yourself to become pessimistic, your experiences will deteriorate, and you will lose the enjoyment you previously possessed.

You must harness the power of your good emotions and resist the destructive emotions that may come your way through the Law of Attraction. This will benefit you in your personal life and your professional life.

In the end, the Law of Attraction is true. It has an impact on people's life. It directly influences how people think, what they say, and, most importantly, what they do.

The Law of Attraction has aided people in overcoming their anxieties, achieving their wishes, meeting the appropriate people, and achieving their goals.

In this brief course, we'll go through how to focus on your vision to live the life of your dreams.

Let's get this party started...

Believe In Your Vision

Now, concentration is more than just a word. It necessitates hard mental lifting. What's the bottom line? The primary purpose of employing the law of attraction in your life is to have faith in your vision.

Believe That It's Possible

First and foremost, you must think that it is doable. Yes, it's feasible that a position in that corner office is available. Yes, it's plausible that this massive estate on the outskirts of the town exists. It's feasible that individuals will be able to grow this great company. Believe in your vision, whatever it is.

This is the foundation of success; you're wasting your effort if you don't think your vision can be realized. You can wind up undermining or sabotaging yourself because you're telling yourself in the back of your mind, "Well, I'm just fooling about with myself. This isn't the real deal. Who

Are you kidding me?" Then everything comes crashing down because you didn't trust in your vision. Believe in yourself and your abilities.

Believe You Can Do It

The next stage is to believe in your ability to succeed. Nobody else, not a friend, a neighbor, a brother, a sister, and a parent, but YOU, individually, can accomplish it.

This places you in the center of the image. You're no longer considering your vision as a speculative exercise. This is no longer a hypothetical situation or something that "would be good" if it happened. Instead, you're smack dab in the center of your life since you're the only one who can do it. That's how you see it.

Believe That Your Vision Is Clear

There is no space for interpretation with a clear vision. There are no blind spots with clear eyesight. Sure, you'll have to fill in some blanks based on your circumstances, but there are no blind spots that will completely surprise you or put you back. Everything is crystal clear, precisely like Michael Phelps' mental movie, which he replays to achieve ultimate victory.

Act-On Your Vision

After that, you must believe in your ability to carry out your vision. This is a critical point. If you think this, it suggests you have the resources or have the ability to obtain them.

It also suggests that now is the ideal moment to act because you can do so. It isn't a hypothetical situation. It's not something that's kept hidden until certain circumstances fall into place at some point in the future that no one knows about. Instead, you feel you can do something about it right now, right here. It doesn't matter if it's a modest step forward or a giant leap; there is something you can do right now.

The following step is critical once you've accomplished that, which is a significant accomplishment. You must think that your vision has already occurred for the Law of Attraction to function for you.

This is where your faith truly takes off because you realize that if you can't get it to this stage, you're simply fooling about and playing games with yourself. You've got to get to this stage. Believe it or not, it has already occurred.

How? It's that easy. If meeting a lovely member of the other sex to be your future spouse or wife is one of your goals, I have some good news for you. Every day, people meet the "right one." Guess what? You may achieve your objective of being a successful businessperson. This is something that a lot of people do.

Allow yourself the power of regularity because the Law of Attraction begins to modify your personal ability to edit your reality when you presume that these things happen regularly. You begin to think differently. You begin to discuss things differently. Your priorities are different from mine. Your

Expectations and assumptions have shifted. As a result, you will make better judgments and take activities to get you closer to your grand vision.

The notion that your vast goal, no matter how high it may appear, has already occurred is a critical step in this direction. You're not trying anything new or out of the ordinary. It's not like you're attempting to raise dragons from the ashes of long-dead stone eggs. You want something to happen; therefore, you're striving towards that.

Help Yourself Out by Using Belief Boosters

I quickly learned that trying to persuade myself into believing particular images based on the Law of Attraction requires much too much effort. It's pretty simple to get depleted. Finally, you feel the burden of the other aspects of your existence, which drains you completely.

I realized that several methods might assist me in enhancing my confidence. When I combine these elements, it creates a powerful combination.

They produce a self-sustaining, belief-boosting, or energizing system, among other things.

Reading Positive Quotes

First, I set out a few minutes each day to read inspirational statements about my vision. They may not be strictly tied to my vision or highly specialized to it, but they are near enough.

These motivational slogans help me keep on track. They remind me that others have accomplished what I'm doing in the past and that they could do so because they were focused. They didn't lose sight of what was important. They didn't lose sight of the prize.

These optimistic quotes, which I repeat repeatedly, begin to penetrate my heart. They become a part of who I am. They become a part of my presumptions.

Make It Part Of Your Daily Routine

Finally, make all of this emphasis a regular part of your day. Spend time on it. "I believe in my vision," consciously state to yourself, and then start thinking about it. Use confidence boosters. You may need to devote a significant amount of time to this step before moving on to the next, but it will be well worth it.

Integrate Your Belief Into Your Daily Life

Much of what you've been doing up to this point has merely engaged your head and emotions. As strong as the human brain and emotions are, you must act on your vision for change in your life

I was able to do this using the following system. I'd read my vision, concentrate on the case studies I'd found, and offer myself affirmations. I would carefully, purposefully, and slowly repeat these affirmations.

I would savor every syllable. I'd make an effort to envision each word. I'd investigate how they interact and what effect they have. I'd find out the many meanings they provide and go into them before incorporating them into my vision.

After everything is apparent, I will erase or shred up my written version of my vision and then rebuild it from memory after a few minutes have passed.

I'm reprogramming my operating system as I go through this process. I'm teaching my mind to ignore uncertainties, self-imposed constraints, unpleasant trauma or negative memories from the past, and pointless future concerns. Rather, I concentrate on my vision.

You should do this first thing in the morning and the last thing at night. This is critical since your mind is immersed in another universe when you sleep. It's cleaning out your memory, but it's also creating a slew of new connections.

If your vision is an important element of that, it will become a part of the reality that your mind creates. The finest aspect is that it happens without our knowledge.

You start behaving a certain way without being able to put your finger on why those changes have happened, but it's actually because of your willful action. It can be traced to the first thing you read and acted on in the morning and the last thing you read and acted on at night.

If you keep doing this, you start to consciously change what you say to yourself. You're no longer calling yourself an idiot. You're staying away from calling yourself a loser or any other negative self-talk.

Just as importantly, you start changing how you talk to others. You no longer say, "I don't have the money," "I can't do it," "Who am I," or "The rich get richer, and the poor get poorer." That goes away. Instead, people start hearing somebody new.

You start talking by planting seeds of life into people's lives instead of weeds like, "I can't do it" or "Who do you think you are," "You have no money," "It's failed before, what makes you think it's going to happen this time around?" All those weeds, I call them mental weeds, start to wither and die, and you start planting seeds of life.

In addition to changes in how you talk, you start changing how you look. You probably have heard the saying, "to make a million bucks, you have to first dress like a million bucks." Well, there's a lot of truth to that because it reflects your self-image. It reflects the type of person you see yourself being.

Again, going back to Michael Phelps, he doesn't see himself as the last guy in the race. Instead, he sees himself as the first guy, winning time after time, all day, every day.

To be a winner, you have to start talking like one. Once you're talking like a winner, it's a good idea to start dressing like one and walking like one. Eventually, you'll start acting like a winner.

But you have to start somewhere. And it all starts in your head. Eventually, it makes this internal change, and reprogramming starts manifesting in how you talk and look, which changes how people perceive you.

If people saw a bum before, and now you show up in an Armani suit, and you treat everybody like a million bucks, what do you think will happen? They will treat you like a million bucks. And soon enough, since you already believe you're a million bucks, and people are saying you're a million bucks, it becomes a reality.

That's how you man up. That's how you step up to the challenge, take life by the ears, and take control.

Importance Of Action And Manifestation

You don't want to seem like a broken record, but I feel compelled to repeat myself. The rest of the world is uninterested with your feelings.. That's something you should think about. Consider that for a moment. It should be carved in stone.

Sure, many people play a nice game around you, attempting to persuade you that your sentiments count, which they do to a degree with your friends and family members. On the other hand, feelings are irrelevant to the rest of the world since everyone has feelings.

You simply have to do one thing if you want the rest of the world to respect you and take you seriously: take action. You transform your universe when you do things because you're now serious. You've shown to the rest of the world that you're not a knucklehead. It's clear that you're serious about it.

What makes it think that? You, on the other hand, have altered your behavior. You've gotten results as a result of your efforts. That is how the rest of the world views you, which gets me to the manifestation step of the Law of Attraction.

This period has spawned a plethora of nonsense novels. Indeed, they are written in such a sloppy and reckless manner that they give the impression that everything is miraculous. There's nothing mystical about it.

About this. Manifestation boils down to believing so much in your vision that it changes your emotional state.

If you can get to this level, the law of attraction is working for you. Why? Once you get to this stage, it's like being on a roller coaster.

If you've ever been on a roller coaster, you know that there is a part of your trip where you go up this steep incline, and then it starts to slow down until a large chunk of the roller coaster is over that hump, and then boom, it goes down at a high rate of speed. That's where you feel like your guts are in your mouth.

Manifestation is getting to that hump because, after that point, the world has no choice but to sit up and pay attention. After all, when you allow your vision, which you have carefully selected, rehearsed, and fine-tuned, to change your emotional state, all bets are off because once your emotions are involved, your actions start to change.

Let your emotional state change your mental habits. This is where you flip the switch from negativity to possibility, from possibility to positivity, and from positivity, you go on to probability. And once you're at that probability stage, congratulations because the change is imminent.

We all start from negativity. At some level or another, we feel we can't do it. We don't have access to the right stuff, and we're not connected, and so forth. There are just tons of toxic excuses that we're stewing in. That's where we start.

But you focus so much on your vision that you can move from negativity to possibility. This is when you start thinking, "Yes, it is possible. It is doable. It's not out of the ordinary. I can't write this off. It can happen."

And then from there, you get to positivity where you feel pumped up that with the right focus, with the right planning, and the right faith, this is going to happen. It's not like it can happen, but it IS going to happen.

And then from there, you go to probability, which is, "I've already put in a lot of time. and the chances of this happening is very high," and then you get to imminent change where you're just inches away. You can smell it. You can feel the heat coming off your vision become real.

Let your changed mental habits lead you to changed actions. Let it happen.

Again, going back to the roller coaster example, when you let your emotional state change your mental habits, it's like you're going over that hump, and after enough of the roller coaster has gone over that hump, you cannot stop the roller coaster because it's going downhill at a crazy rate of speed. That's what makes it so terrifying and fun at the same time.

That's exactly what happens once you make the switch to that emotional state because it becomes harder and harder to stop this chain reaction until you let your changed mental habits lead to changed actions. Let it happen. Stop doubting yourself. Give up on second-guessing yourself. Let it happen.

It may seem like it will take time but find the time. Eventually, you will look at your daily actions to achieve your big goals in life through the power of the Law of Attraction as a reward, in and of itself. If you reach that point, congratulations because you are well on your way to living an unstoppable life

CONFIDENCE UNSHAKEABLE

Introduction

Have you been thinking of ways to grow your confidence? Do you feel that fear has taken over a huge part of your life and is holding you back from living your true purpose? Do you want to shake all that fear and have unstoppable confidence that will leave people in awe of you? Well, this book is designed just for you!

Today, so many of us are not living up to our full potential due to the fear of failure or what others will think of us. That is one of the most common regrets most people have when near their deathbed. You have to understand that fear will take away the sunshine in your life and leave you with so much darkness and sadness within.

The good news is that you can shake all that fear and self-judgment so that you take control of your life and live a purposeful and happy life. The one way to do this is to master the art of confidence. Through authentic confidence, you lay a solid foundation for making better decisions, building long-lasting relationships, and positioning yourself for success.

What Comes To Mind When You Think Of Confidence?

"Happiness is when what you think, what you say, and what you do are in harmony." – Mahatma Gandhi.

This is exactly what I think serves as a recipe for confidence. If you are going to live a fulfilled life, you must have the confidence to go after the things that make you happy. In other words, you have to demonstrate confidence in yourself, abilities, personality, and intellect.

So, what is confidence? Well, the truth about unshakeable confidence is living true to yourself. It is all about embracing your true self. To do this, you must believe that you have full control of your life and not let circumstances hinder you from your life purpose. You have to decide the value of your true self and never allow yourself to be defined by someone else's opinion. The more you do this, the more it becomes effortless to express confidence.

When you master the art of embracing your true self, you will realize that the doors of opportunity are all around you. You will be spoilt for choices. There is no more room for fear of scarcity when limitless opportunities come your way. Soon, you'll

Realize that you can live a life of abundance. This is exactly what I consider an effective pathway to unshakeable confidence and a fulfilled life.

CHAPTER 1: THREE PILLARS OF UNSHAKEABLE CONFIDENCE

Pillar 1: Experiential Confidence

Chatting up with females, especially strangers, was one of the things that scared me as a kid. It was tough to make the first approach, and I felt as if my feet had completely lost their force. To put it another way, it prompted me to shut down!

Now, two decades later, I'm still baffled about what I was so terrified of.

Because we now have experience, you and I can easily overcome fear and achieve things that we once believed were impossible. I was able to push through those nerve-wracking conversations and times. I can now strike up a conversation with everyone I come across, whether it's on the subway, at a coffee shop, or work.

I am confident in accomplishing almost whatever I set my mind to. It's similar to the first time you learned to drive on the highway. It was frightening at first, but you adjust, and your body learns that it does not harm you.

Experiential confidence is a term used to describe this type of confidence. It's the kind of self-assurance that comes with experience. You have attained this degree of self-assurance at some point in your life. The first stage is to summon the guts to take action and risk. Each time you fail, you gain confidence in yourself because you realize that failure isn't permanent.

One thing you should be grateful for in your life is all the things that did not work out because they taught you something. We have trust now because of previous failures. As a result, if you want to improve your experience confidence, the first question you should ask yourself is, "What is the worst that may happen if I fail?" Will you perish? There is no need to back down if this is not the case. You must understand that every action you do in the face of fear increases your experienced confidence, and all actions that are tough today will become simple eventually.

Pillar 2: Emotional Confidence

This simply refers to the level of confidence that you can switch on and off at will. For example, at the age of 21, I began working as a project assistant for an international corporation. For whatever reason, I once desired to work from a different city for three weeks. However, I was terrified of approaching my employer and asking for permission to work outside the main office. Is it true that I completed the task? Definitely.

So, first and foremost, I had to psychologically prepare myself. I began by visualizing how I would enter his office, make my case, and respond to his comments. I made a little decision tree with all of the conceivable ifs, hows, and whys he'd ask, as well as my replies. This was to keep me on my toes and make sure nothing caught me off guard. To put it another way, I needed this to keep my cool.

I was ultimately learning how to tap into my emotional confidence by learning how to regulate my body language so that I didn't convey the wrong impression. If you can manage your body, you'll control your emotions. If you don't have control of your body, on the other hand, your emotions will be all over the place.

I just practiced every remark I was going to make and how I would deliver it, with a strong handshake, a smile on my face, and my shoulders up. When you resist the impulse to cross your arms and display your uneasiness, the conversation flows easily, and the other person eases into the conversation. That is how you develop emotional self-assurance.

It's vital to remember that emotional confidence comes in handy when you're faced with a circumstance you've anticipated, such as a presentation, a difficult chat with your boss or parents, a performance, and so on. Emotional confidence, unlike experiential confidence, is not restricted to a particular area.

The only issue here is that emotional confidence does not come naturally. To activate it, you must connect with your inner self.

But what do you do when you're in such a terrible circumstance and don't feel like it? We'll get into more detail on how to stand up for yourself and deal with difficult circumstances.

Pillar 3: Self-Esteem

This is the deepest confidence level and is the true definition of unshakeable confidence! One mistake that people make today is thinking that confidence has everything to do with survival. The tough truth is that there are so many people with huge muscles, decorated war veterans, and even firefighters who do not have self-confidence! They do not have the confidence to initiate a conversation with a stranger. You have to understand that confidence is something that is broken by identity and not broken bones in this time and age.

We often think to ourselves... What if others hate me? What if I gave the presentation and they ignored me?

What would people think of me? These are all self-defeating questions.

To achieve strong self-esteem, you must first ensure that your genuine identity is linked to your beliefs and ideals. It all begins with you recognizing and accepting that the only person who can destroy your identity is you!

Developing high self-esteem simply implies that you have the highest level of self-assurance since your identity is intact. Instead, you create your persona. You must never allow others to define your identity or purpose for you. You have the ability and desire to follow your code.

When you cease feeling like your identity is on the line, you'll know you're confident. There is no rejection, strangeness, or public humiliation that can distress you if you live up to your standards. So, what measures do we need to take to live a life of high standards and unrivaled confidence? Some of these include giving it your all, completely expressing yourself, accepting responsibility for your happiness, and constantly aiming to do the right thing rather than the easy thing.

It makes no difference what other people think. If you live by this motto, you will never be at the mercy of other people's ideas. Allow your mission to be your guiding light at all times, and always give it you're all. Don't be scared to do the things that make you nervous, and give it you're all! With this mindset, there is no way to lose. You will get far more than you could have dreamed.

There's an adage that says, "familiarity creates comfort." If you're going to a meeting, make sure you expose yourself to scenarios that give you a sense of familiarity. If you're going to a meeting, run through the schedule in your head. If you're giving a presentation, go through it in your brain first.

It is also vital that you get control over your emotions. To properly break out that nasty mood, fear, or pattern, take at least three minutes and talk loudly, with a grin on your face, while taking slow and deep breaths into your belly. You will realize that no failure, rejection, or humiliation will disturb your genuine identity if you make this your identity.

CHAPTER 2: THE SECRET LANGUAGE OF ROCK-SOLID CONFIDENT PEOPLE

Here are the three most powerful secrets of Rock-Solid Confident People:

They Manage Their Minds At Every Moment

People who have rock-solid confidence know how to manage their minds at every moment. You feel overly anxious about that job interview, presentation, or performance because you can't manage your mindset well to handle the tasks.

The beauty of our mindset is that we can easily choose to shift it at any time towards the direction we choose. Let us consider an example of relaxing in your home on Saturday.

Morning having breakfast with your loved ones. Suddenly, the phone rings. Out of nowhere, you were told that you must attend an urgent meeting in an hour! And you have to abandon your family for this unexpected meeting elsewhere.

Wow! Anyone in their right mind will feel ambushed, angry, and anxious being put in such a situation. However, all you have to do is instantly shift your focus from enjoying family time to getting into the confident, high-level meeting mindset.

Nobody said that this would be easy because it is not. But the first thing you should do is try and gather information from your boss about the expectations of the meeting, the schedule, the stakeholders seating in the meeting, and other important details. You could then talk to your family about what just happened and get going.

The thing that is very important to note is that when a new, unexpected situation arises, you have to accept that you will feel frustrated, challenged, and stressed out. However, you can trick your brain into the right state of mind and get the important things done right away. At first, this may not be easy. However, as you gain more knowledge and learn from experience, you will always be mentally prepared for this unexpected event.

Simply ask yourself whether there is anything at all that will get you in the right frame of mind. Think of your brain like Google, in which anything you ask will be answered.

They Start A "Dream Factory."

If you are going to have confidence in life, the key to having a sense of direction in which your life is growth. A simple question such as, "What would you like your life to be like?" is enough to help you put things into perspective. Determine what your dream lifestyle is like and how you measure your level of success. Then write all your responses on a piece of paper.

Ideally, you should get up each morning and read this paper about your dream life and take a few minutes to visualize it. As days go by, you can add more specifics to your dream life. By starting the day in such a way, you imprint rock-solid confidence into your subconscious mind. This will also inform what steps you take to bring you closer to your dream life.

They Intentionally halt Giving A Hoot About What Others Think Of Them.

If you desire rock-solid confidence, you have to come to terms with the fact that people will always judge. This means that the only person that you really should be impressing is you! Unshakeable confidence comes from setting your expectations and then giving your all to live up to them. You stand to gain nothing when you match your goals with other people's expectations.

Well, don't get me wrong, healthy competition isn't bad! When you have great motivators in life, you will always work hard and model your successes. If you are an athlete and you managed to beat your all-time best record. Even though you might have come in second in a race, you should not be disappointed because you have done your best and broke your record. That is all that matters.

Every single day, purposefully do the right thing and give it your best, and then go ahead and be proud of the person you are. If you have a Hard desire to quit your job and start a business to pursue your dreams, then, by all means, do it! It does not matter what people think. All that matters is that you are running your race for the ultimate prize- your dream life!

That said, having rock-solid confidence is not an easy task. You have to learn to shut out all the external noise so that you can listen to your inner voice. If you always live your pleasing others, you will never confidently pursue your dreams but live a miserable life. A life of regret is a life that we should always stay away from. Unshakeable confidence comes when you stop being controlled by people and rather take control of your own life and steer it in the direction you want to go.

DREAM IT
WISH IT
DO IT

Freshly Brewed
Classic Italian Coffee

BEERS OF THE WORLD

SDP

Live
LOVE
Laugh

Bear Lodge

How Great would life be
if we lived a little of it
★ ——Everyday—— ★

YOU ARE SO
WORTH IT

friends
are the stars
that light up
your life

LOVE

ENJOY THIS DAY
Be present
BREATHE DEEPLY
Show gratitude
Live with intention
BE FEARLESS
TRY NEW THINGS

MY
KIDS
HAVE
PAWS

WELCOME
LIVE
LOVE laugh

YOGA CLASS?
I THOUGHT YOU SAID
POUR A GLASS

when nothing
goes right...
Go Left

COUNT YOUR
BLESSINGS

BE
kind
to
one
another

WAKE UP
SAY A PRAYER
AND HUSTLE

LIFE
BEGINS
AFTER
COFFEE

EVERYDAY
is a fresh start

GOOD MOMS HAVE
STICKY FLOORS,
DIRTY OVENS,
AND HAPPY KIDS.

HAPPY
WIFE
HAPPY
LIFE

Never
stop
making
wishes

DREAMS
DON'T
WORK
UNLESS
YOU DO

THIS IS
OUR
HAPPY
PLACE

BLISS
in
BLOOMS

good
friends
are
like
st

Family
is all the
love you need

SLIDE

HOME

Live them

IF YOUR DREAMS
DON'T SCARE YOU
THEY'RE NOT BIG ENOUGH

All our dreams
can come true

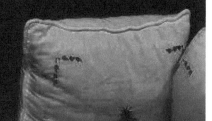

CHAPTER 3: STEPS TO BUILDING AN UNSHAKEABLE CONFIDENCE

Step 1: Step Out from Your Comfort Zone

You must be willing to step outside of your comfort zone to do things out of the ordinary if you want to have unwavering confidence. It would be best if you rekindled the desire to be extraordinary that has been burning within you.

Maybe you have a brilliant idea that you think would benefit your company, but you're unsure how to tell your boss about it. Perhaps you've always had a crush on someone you've never dared to approach.

The problem with not acting on these desires is that you will remain stuck in the same place. The truth is that when you refuse to try new things, you are allowing fear to steal your sunshine. You're just digging deeper into your comfort zone.

Comfort. You've been sitting in this hole for decades.

Yes, stepping into the unknown for the first time can be intimidating, especially if you don't want to be embarrassed if you fail. Because once you think about it, it all comes down to 'FEAR,' which is for False Evidence Appearing Real. What are the worst- case scenarios? Frequently, you are simply overthinking. Leaving your comfort zone might be terrifying, but it's necessary if you want to achieve your life's mission and have unwavering confidence. This could be your chance to show yourself that you can accomplish anything you set your mind to.

After all, what could go wrong? You have the option of sharing with your employer and steering the firm to success, or the boss might decline. Visitors could offer that girl or boy out, and then they could say yes or no, and you'd know right away without simply assuming. In either event, it's a definite plus.

You are the key to having unwavering self-assurance!

I can guarantee that if you want to go out of your comfort zone, you must first create micro-goals that will gradually add to the broader picture. Micro-goals are minor components of a more significant objective that you have. Breaking down larger goals into smaller portions makes them easier to achieve.

It's pretty simple, and you'll have a great time doing it.

This will also encourage you to keep going till you achieve your goal.

Let's return to the case we discussed previously. So, you've got a company concept or plan you'd want to share with your employer but lack the bravery to do so. Instead, you might break down your main aim into smaller objectives that eventually provide comparable results. Start with modest steps, no matter how insignificant. Starting small will relieve the strain of taking the big stage and feeling overwhelmed. You make things easier to absorb and follow up on when.

So you have no confidence to tell that girl or boy how you feel. However, they could not be single to begin with. So, before you get into the deep end of things, your micro objective should be to create a rapport with them. Please call to know who they are even before you ask them out on a date by starting a brief chat with them. Isn't that a step forward? This doesn't sound like you're following them around.

However, it would help if you recognized that setting micro-goals allows you to venture outside your comfort zone. As you achieve your micro-goals one by one, you'll notice that they're all interconnected.

Small victories might give you the confidence you need to take the next step. Challenge yourself to do something out of the usual every day and notice how your confidence increases as a result.

Step 2: Know Your Worth

Did you know that persons with a strong sense of self-assurance are typically quite decisive? Successful individuals have in common that they do not waste time attempting to make tiny judgments. Said they don't overthink things. They can make quick judgments because they already know the larger picture or the result.

But how do you define your desires?

The first step for you to do is to determine your values. According to author Tony Robbins, there are two deals: end values and means discounts. These two categories of matters are tied to the emotional state you want to achieve, such as happiness, security, and satisfaction.

Means Values

These relate to methods for eliciting the desired feeling. Money, for example, is frequently used as a means rather than an aim. It will provide you with financial independence, something you want, and hence has capital worth.

Ends Values

This relates to the emotions you're seeking, such as love, happiness, and safety. They're just the benefits that your financial resources provide. For example, money will give you financial security and stability.

Put another way, and value is what you believe you want to reach the end values. The most valuable thing is to understand what you value to make better-informed decisions. As a result, you'll have a strong sense of self and be able to draw steadfast confidence from it. You must be in command of your life rather than the other way around.

One way to achieve this is to define your end values. To begin, set aside at least an hour or two each day.

Take a week to put out your desired outcomes. To get there, start by articulating what values you'd like to cultivate to achieve your ideal existence.

- What is one of the most precious things in your life?

- Which are some of the essential things in your life?

- Are there any aspects of your life that you are uninterested in?

- What principles will you uphold, and which ones would you abandon if you have to make a difficult decision?

- What values would you teach your children if you have or have had children?

Step 3: Be Ready To Embrace Change

Have you ever been preoccupied with the future or the past? This is something that many of us do regularly. But here's the thing: the person you were five years ago or will be five years from now is not the same as the person you are now.

You'll note that your tastes, hobbies, and friends were different five years ago than they are now, and they are likely to be added five years from now. The key is to accept who you are now and recognize that you are a living organism.

According to Carol Dweck's study, students who adopt a development mindset do well. They feel that they can excel in a particular area because they have a development mentality. This is the polar opposite of what youngsters with a fixed perspective go through since they feel that everything they are and have is permanent. As a result, believing that you can't progress serves to stifle your self-assurance.

Stopping self-judgment is the first step toward embracing all of who you are. We spend most of our time assessing individuals based on what they say, how they say it, what they dress, and how they act. Similarly, we judge ourselves in our brains by comparing our previous and current selves.

It would be best to begin by breaking the habit of self-judgment and negative criticism to establish a strong feeling of confidence. Yes, it may appear challenging at first, but you'll realize how backward it was after you begin training.

You might begin by committing to at least one or two days per week when you will refrain from making any judgments. Don't say anything if you don't have anything positive to say. If a terrible idea enters your head, you immediately replace it with a good one. Your mind will gradually begin to prime itself to a state of non- judgment, and it will quickly become your standard frame of thought. This will not only help you accept others, but it will also help you accept yourself for who you are.

Step 4: Be Present

Isn't it straightforward? It would be good if you increased your self-assurance. You are simply allowing your mind, body, and soul to be engaged in the task at hand when you are present.

Let's pretend you're talking to someone who isn't paying attention to what you're saying. This is undoubtedly something that has occurred to many of us. How did you feel at the time? Consider conversing with someone and feeling as if you were the only person in the room. Isn't it something special?

The fact that they were present at the time makes you feel unique. They were paying great attention to everything you said.

I'm experiencing every emotion beside you. They were more deeply involved in the discourse. You may retain facts while still feeling empathy in this way.

You must develop a mental double-check to be present. This means that you should check in with yourself regularly. To do so, you'll need to create a mental trigger or calendar for when you're wondering where your mind is. This is the period when you operate as a mental spectator.

While you're at a meeting, are you considering making dinner reservations? Do you always feel as though you're not good enough? To mentally check in on yourself and call yourself out of these negative thoughts necessitates that you do so.

Consider taking care of yourself frequently. Take a deep breath and refocus your concentration on your most critical obligations once you have the answer to your query.

CHAPTER 4: STICKING UP FOR YOURSELF

Most people do not know how to stand up for themselves when caught up in a fix. Some people will always be waiting for your downfall and crushing your confidence if you do not stick up for what you believe in. If you want to live a life with unshakeable beliefs, start by learning how to stand up for yourself.

Before You Can Confront, Be Certain Of What You Want

This is the very first step; knowing what you want. When people come attacking you from all sides, what do you want as the outcome? Do you want them to stop being disrespectful? Is it their specific behavior you do not like? When you know what you want from a situation or what intentions you

Have you will have the power to control the situation and not let the situation get out of hand.

Have Clarity On Your Response & Understand The 'Truth'

You have to note that how you respond is derived from your filter, experience, and understanding that others have the right to hold a different opinion. If you take the time to understand that truth, you will know that you can't always change others but only change how you see things from within. Accepting that will set you free from feeling intimidated by other people's behavior.

Nevertheless, the point is not about being desperate for someone else's approval. It is about you ensuring that before you can confront anyone, you clearly know what values you stand for and that your integrity is firmly grounded.

Release Any Attachment

We have discussed previously that it is essential that you know what you want, why you want it, and how you perceive other people's expectations. Also, you must understand that you cannot expect someone else to change for you.

Therefore, rather than betting your happiness on others, accept that behaviors are hard to change and let go of any attachment. It is usual for everyone to want an unhealthy situation to change. However, betting your happiness on them changing is a losing bet.

Write It Out Before You Talk

This is as simple as it is. There are so many things that people will do or say that will make you angry. However, what truly matters is ensuring that you do not allow that anger to develop into an attack.

"The truth doesn't attack."

–Danielle LaPorte

Create Some Time To Have A Talk

Well, there is always that desire to put someone in their rightful place, something that works perfectly well in movies. However, in reality, this does not come as a beneficial strategy. The best means by which you can cause a shift in your relationship is by having an honest talk with them. The actual address is not about talking down on others verbally, it's more about having a mature conversation.

Stop Talking

This is probably something that many consider a sign of weakness. In this case, knowing when to stop talking is a form of self-confidence. It is a sign that you are grounded with your principles, standards, and values and do not allow others to define who you are. You know your true identity, and you do not need to prove yourself to others and beg for validation.

Rather than wasting your time and energy trying to engage with people who are stubborn with their own opinion, the biggest favor you can do for yourself is walk away. This is a move that only genuinely confident people do because they know what is important to them, what they want, and treasure their time.

With unshakeable confidence, you realize that your time is far too precious to waste on people who do not respect themselves and others. If they cannot appreciate the people around them, you know that they are not the kind of people you want to waste your time on.

If you try to take them down, you will not feel any better. You have to understand that sticking up for yourself does not always happen.

Mean that you have to win. Walk away so that you create more space and time for the people that will embrace, accept, and honor you the way you are. This is the ultimate path of those with unshakeable confidence.

CHAPTER 5: ACTIONABLE TIPS & EXERCISES TO CONSOLIDATE YOUR CONFIDENCE

Grow Your Knowledge

Learning as much as you can both at home and work is the first step in becoming more confident. There is always a part of you that you think you don't know as much about or understand as well as you should.

If you want to have more confidence, you have to demonstrate mastery in this area. You can expand your knowledge by taking online courses, attending similar conferences and events, as well as reading books. The other thing that you can enjoy while gaining knowledge is teleclasses, where you get to interact and engage in discussions with your peers. This will go a long way in improving your level of confidence.

Experience And Celebrate Small Victories

Unshakeable confidence comes from the ability to experience and celebrate small victories and successes. Think of this as giving rewards for applying knowledge. Remember when we discussed micro-goals? Well, now, each time you achieve a micro- goal, you reward yourself. They are not the ultimate big goal, but small chunks make up the bigger goal.

The compensation doesn't have to be big to be good... If you get a pat on the back or a compliment from a coworker, that's enough to make you feel better about yourself. Because of this, make sure you keep track of each small success and thoroughly enjoy it. People who feel more confident every day will start to do things that make them feel more confident.

Exercise Passionate Faith

One of the things I like about confident people is that they believe in a supreme being. That's what they think. They think the creator of the universe has a reason for every living thing. In other words, the reason we're on this planet now is to find out and do our best work.

In other words, they seem to have perfect knowledge that when they forge through with the creator's plan, achieving success is just a matter of time. Therefore, if you genuinely want to achieve success, you must have faith that it is possible. You must have unwavering faith in your potential. When your faith is filled with passion, then there is a high likelihood that you will follow your true purpose.

Enable A Firm Resolve

Naturally, you will face setbacks and disappointments along the way in this life. It's normal to be angry and discouraged, so that's why. However, you must see these setbacks as a chance to learn. Start seeing your setbacks as a setup for something bigger yet to happen in your future.

When you express faith in your abilities, you will get past discouragements and gain a firm resolve. It is this resolve that will, in turn, help you overcome obstacles. This is mainly because firm resolve is a true mark of patience at work. Rather than despairing, you will realize that without these challenges, you would not have a growth mindset. You must ensure that your mind is focused on the intended outcome and not on roadblocks. Instead of thinking of a thousand reasons why you can't, think of one reason why you can.

With time, you will see your talents grow into abilities. It is only then that you will begin to see what is truly possible, a measure of success steering you forward with so much vigor and enthusiasm. It is this enthusiasm that will keep you fired up to keep scoring those small micro-goals.

Enlist Expert Help

Find places where you don't know as much as you should and learn more about them. Once you do that, ask for help from people who can help you learn more and get more experience. When you know that experts are there to help you, you will also be more confident when you take action and make decisions... You can learn from the experts from books, blogs, videos, phone calls, one-on-one meetings, seminars, etc. The good thing with a professional coach is that they will help you remain accountable for every action you take in completing your plans.

Note that if you want unshakeable confidence, you have to attract confidence. Yes, experts will show you the way, but they will not walk the path for you. You have to be willing to go through all obstacles with your head held high and keep your eyes on the prize. Eventually, you will get there.

Visualize Confidence

Its more comfortable knowing you can make yourself look, the more likely you are to be confident in real life, too. Take a moment to picture yourself having the confidence you need in a certain situation.

Imagine how that would make you feel and act as though you already have that confidence. If possible, close your eyes and see yourself using your mind's eye, working with so much confidence and conviction. Keep that picture in your mind, and you will realize that your vision will begin taking root and becoming a reality.

Expect To Be Confident

Exactly do you know that faith in action is based on what you expect? When you think about being confident, you have already thought about how it would make you feel. Optimism means that you will be more confident when you talk, act, and move. You will also be more excited when you work toward your goals. This is when you know that you can see, feel, and act like someone confident. In other words, you will be in a better position to do better than you thought you could. When you think you're going to be confident, it becomes a fact.

Like we have already said, confidence is not something that happens overnight. You have to put these actionable tips into practice for months constantly. Start by writing down ways you intend to apply these action plans. This way, you know exactly what it would be like to take action towards your goal. When you act on them, you start realizing tremendous improvements in your confidence, and soon this translates to unshakeable confidence, happiness, joy, and ultimate success in life.

DEVELOPING COURAGE

CONFIDENCE UNSHAKEABLE

Introduction

" This one is not born with boldness, but one is born with a lot of potentials. . This is true." Without courage, we can't keep up with any other virtue. There is no way to be kind or true or merciful or generous.

Some people don't dare to face all of the problems that come their way. Lucky are the people who take risks and get through all the problems. As others have said, courage is not built-in. This allows them to face their fears, take risks without losing faith, and live even when hard. Everyone has a certain amount of this, so they can do this.

Everyone wants courage. It is a trait of good character that makes someone worth respecting. During this book, you'll learn about courage and how to use it in your life. So, don't miss this chance to learn more about courage and the benefits of having enough courage to win any fight.

CHAPTER 1: AN OVERVIEW OF COURAGE

Synopsis

Everything scares people in some way. But, being brave can help you face or overcome your fears in life, even if that means giving up or taking risks. There is no need to be scared of Everything in life. Life will never run out of things to do. People already have them in their lives. That's why you dare to win any fights in life. How have you dealt with every fear that has come your way since you were little? You have to have the courage or your instincts.

Courage Defined

Courage is the strength to face pain, fear, uncertainty, intimidation, or danger. You can have a lot of different kinds of courage, from endurance and physical strength to mental strength and new ideas. Some types of courage:

Physical Courage

This is the courage that comes when you have to deal with hardship, pain, or even death or death.

Moral Courage

If a person can do the right thing even when other people don't like them, there is a lot of gossip, and they're discouraged or ashamed; this is called "courage."

People in some cultures think of courage and fortitude as the same thing. In Western thought, the most important ideas about courage came from philosophers like Aquinas, Aristotle, and Kierkegaard. There are a lot of ideas about courage in the Tao Te Ching, which is a book in the East. Recently, the psychology field looked into courage.

6 Attributes of Courage

Everyone wants courage. In a lot of stories and even movies, you've seen it. The truth is, history books have taught everyone how to be brave and brave. Courage comes in many forms. But, you should work on more of it, because this can give you an advantage and lead to success, so you should do that more. Make sure you know what courage is made up of if you think you don't dare to do something. These are:

Feeling Fear Yet You Choose to Act

Several people are afraid of something, but most of you choose to do something instead of letting your fear get the best of you. Courage is not the absence of fear. And although, you have to get over your fears, as well. Think about how true courage comes when you're afraid.

Following Your Heart

All of your dreams may not be possible. On the other hand, this world has a limited time, and you need to follow your heart. This is what you call courage.

Standing Up For What Is Right

Only a small number of people are brave enough to speak out against injustice and injustice—those who speak out for what is right need a lot of courage. Courage will also show you when it's best to sit and listen.

There are other qualities of courage, too, but this is the most important one. To become braver, you should start today. Everyone can improve their courage. Your courage can be your best weapon when you fight your enemies and other things that get in the way.

Courage is not simply one of the virtues, but the form of every virtue at the testing point — C.S. Lewis

CHAPTER 2: IDENTIFY YOUR STRENGTHS

Synopsis

You need to be good at things if you want to do well at something. In this life, you might not be able to face the challenges if you don't know your strengths. not the things you think are good at. Because you are good at something, this doesn't mean that it is your strength. Strength should also be your favorite thing. This makes it a strength of yours, so you can use it. How can you figure out your strengths?

Ways to Know Your Strengths

Your strengths will help you become braver. Strength makes you feel strong. People often get mixed up between their strengths and weaknesses. Here are some ideas:

List Down What You Think You Are Good At

To figure out your strengths, write down what you think you are good at. Even though you don't like it yet, you're good at it, which could be your strength. It will support you in the long run if you write down Everything you're good at. When Knowing Your Strengths, Don't Ask Opinions from Other People.

When you know your strengths, it's not a good idea to ask other people for their thoughts. You know more about yourself than anyone else does. So, don't let other people influence you when you find out your strengths because your real strength is inside you. This is why you should be the one who knows your strengths, not someone else.

There are several reasons why you should not solicit the opinions of others. Many people might just think you're good at something because you do it well. But they don't know how you feel about it. What Makes You Excited

Everyone has his or her excitement in life. So, what makes you excited? Being excited about something you plan to do can be your strength. You have to note that you should have passion for what you do to be a strength. Sometimes when you enjoy doing and do very well at it, this is your strength. Take Some Self-Assessment Activities

There are many ways to find out what your strengths are. One way to do this is to do some self-assessment activities. Some experts or professionals give these things away for free. To do any self-assessment activity you want, just go ahead and do it! Make sure this will let you know your strengths.

They could be a waste of time for other people. But, some people who aren't sure where to start might think about these activities. You might also be able to figure out your weaknesses through self-assessment activities. You can work on them in the long run, and they might become one of your strengths in the process. Keep in mind that some of your flaws can help you get better at something. Know how to use it well. Signs of Power

Another way to know how strong you are is to pay attention to the signs that your strength gives off. These signs are:

Success

This shows that you are good at what you are doing. Instincts

Look for things that make you excited. Then, make the most of them.

Growth

You grow when you focus on one thing, and time moves quickly. Needs

Many things could make you tired, but they will make you happy.

The following step is to increase your abilities. As long as you work to improve your strengths, they will only be a strength to you. If you don't think about it, this could be your weakness in the long run.

There are many things you can do to help your strengths grow. In one way, you can use your skills by getting involved in things that allow you to do so. The more you do this, the better you will improve your skills, even if you think your rivals are better than you. So, don't waste your time on something that doesn't value your skills. Nurture your strengths and enjoy the benefits that come with them.

CHAPTER 3: THINK POSITIVELY

Synopsis

Keepin' your head up isn't a simple job. Most of the time, people encourage negative thoughts, especially if they are angry and can't handle things right. But, what they don't know is that negative thinking will only make things more complicated and will never lead anyone to the right path, so they should stop thinking that way. There is always a solution in math, and it could be right around the corner. Thinking positively, on the other hand, can help you keep going. There is no matter how hard they are. This will give you the strength to win any fight, no matter how hard it is.

How to Think Positively If Things Go Wrong in Life

Even though your life seems to be falling apart, you need to think positively even if you don't feel things are going well. Is there someone you have looked at and wondered how they could be so happy all the time? Their positive attitude and outlook on life set them apart from the rest. If you think optimistically, you can attain your life goals. Because being optimistic when things go wrong can also help you have a lot less stress in your life, here are some things you may do:

People don't merely go through the motions of life. They figure out a way to live them out. Each day should be lived as if it were your last. Everyone who has a strong sense of purpose and a good outlook on life will aspire to be like them. Some people like to be in the company of joyful people.

Make sure you don't become enraged and instead focus on your work. Don't wait if something goes wrong. Take command of your life and make things happen for yourself. You won't move forward if you're too angry or scared in this situation. Make your own life. You only get one chance. So, enjoy life as it comes. Then, make the most of what you have.

Don't stop believing, no matter what happens. Everything happens for a reason. As long as things seem bad now, there is always a chance they could turn out for the better in the long run.

Draw strength from your bad luck. People who think positively even if things go wrong will get through it. Be thankful for the things you have. Those who are successful know that being grateful will get them a lot farther than being unhappy. There is nothing wrong with having a goal. You should also thank yourself for what you have right now. People who aren't happy or content will think that they won't get what they want.

When chances come your way, take them. Do not let your responsibilities get in the way of pursuing your dreams, but don't pass up the opportunities that will work best for your life.

Laugh at yourself. Everyone wants to be with people who can laugh even when having a bad day. Smile or laugh at yourself when you make mistakes. This is one way to think positively.

Remember that you are the only one who can change your fate. No one can stop you from having dreams except you. As long as you aren't dead, there is still hope. It doesn't matter how bad things are in your life right now. You still have a lot.

He or she isn't doing anything in their life at the moment. Besides, why not? Then, make it the life that you want.

Even when things aren't going as well as you'd like, it's hard to think positively. But, it isn't impossible. These tips will help you get on the right track.

The following are some other ways to help you think more positively.

Other things that can help you think more positively:

Set Goals that are SMART.

If you don't know what you want to do in life, you won't know where you're going. But, if you set clear goals, you will be happy. So, set your goals and have a good attitude.

Form a picture in your mind of how you'll do well.

Forming a mental picture of your success may be a waste of time. That's not all. This can help you achieve all your goals. As a point, you will also be more likely to achieve the things you want in life.

Take charge and ownership of your own life.

Do not blame other people or problems for your problems or problems. Do not let yourself be a victim of someone else. As the captain of your boat, you decide where it goes. Start making a new plan right away if you aren't happy with your life.

When you fail, make up for it.

If Everything else doesn't work, then think about faking it. As if you are confident and self-assured, you can act nervous, worried, or unsure. It's important to smile and act as though you're professional, successful, and happy. You can fool other people and your brain. Make sure to do this because you already know how it feels to be happy at Everything.

Remove the Negative

Use positive self-talk to fight off the negative thoughts and doubts in your head. You can get rid of your worries about obstacles and difficulties by thinking positively. There are things you should not do when there is a problem in your life. You need to face them to be brave.

Negative thinking may be an easy choice because it's more comfortable and doesn't require as much work. Don't fall for this. Think positive because this can help you build up your courage and be braver.

CHAPTER 4: ANALYZE AT ALL POINTS OF VIEW

Synopsis

One's point of view is how he or she thinks about a certain story. Everyone has their ideas about life. Everyone's point of view may change depending on how they have grown or what they have learned in the past. For example, if you are always around people who have a positive attitude and don't let negative thoughts get in the way when things go wrong, you will become more optimistic. It's also possible that you'll always be negative about what you do. If two people have different points of view, that can affect. To be brave, you need to look at all sides.

Why Is It Important to Look at All the Ways to Build Courage?

It can be hard to deal with the problems that come up every day in the life. You need to be brave enough to fight and get over these kinds of things. When you look at other people's points of view, you learn how to be brave. You are the one who is facing the obstacle, not them. So why should you look at all sides?

There are several reasons to consider things from a different perspective. Things aren't always seen in the same light by everyone. Life may be simple in some ways and difficult in others, even if many around you believe it is simple. You stand out because you are different from everyone else. So, if you're having a difficult time right now, consider what others have done to get through it.

People with different points of view are important because they help you see the bright side of things even though other people think it's already the end of the world for them. Instead of giving up, you will be motivated and inspired to get through the situation because you believe you can do it.

The Benefits of Looking at All the Ways People See the Same Things

It's possible that viewing from every angle isn't worth your attention. However, several positive outcomes might occur as a result of your actions:

Be able to separate your current situation from that of others. One of the best things about looking at Everything from different angles is seeing how your situation is different from other people's. It's not the same for people from different walks of life to deal with.

A lot of things can be hard, but some can be simple. But, once you're in a certain situation and think you can't do it, you should think again and compare your situation to others in the same situation as you. This can make a big difference.

Other People's points of view can be a source of motivation or inspiration for you, too.

Another benefit of looking at all points of view is that you can use other people's perspectives as inspiration or motivation to do better. If you don't have courage, think about people who work hard to win their battles in life and fight against any injustice. Instead of giving up, why not use different points of view to motivate and inspire people to do good things instead? Anybody can bring you down as long as you dare to cope with a problem.

In your mind, you may think that it is hard to make other people's ideas your motivation or inspiration. But the process is simple. You don't have to change yourself to be brave like other people. Make sure you act just like them. By putting their good traits into your system, you will be able to be as brave as they are.

You'll know what you should and should not do.

You can also be aware of what you should or should not do if you look at things differently. If you think your situation is hopeless, look at what others have done. With this, you can figure out which things you should put first.

Having a better understanding of what you're facing

Most of the time, people think they are at their worst if they have some problems. They don't understand what they are going through better. Things happen for a reason, and you need the courage to face any obstacle that comes your way.

Being Able to Make the Right Decisions.

Some people struggle to take appropriate action because they don't know when or where to begin. By looking at Everything, anyone can act wisely because they already know how other people try their best to deal with the problems that come their way.

You can think more positively when you do this.

When things go wrong, looking at Everything will help you figure out why. Only if you take risks and don't think about the bad things that could happen will you know that life can be better. You will be able to think positively because of the past experiences of some people. This can help you go in the right direction.

You get to see things from other people's points of view, which is a good thing. Don't forget about the things above if you want to have enough courage. They can make a big difference.

CHAPTER 5: USE SPIRITUALLY TO CONNECT

Synopsis

Having the courage to face many trials in your life can let you stay on track despite the difficulties. But, without spirituality, most of you might lose faith in fighting. This is the main reason you should also pay importance to the value of spirituality to have true courage.

Spiritualism is the search for something sacred and important that people should consider. People approach spirituality by meditation, religion, personal reflection, or yoga.

Reasons Why Spirituality Is Needed to Be Courageous

Others don't believe that spirituality has something to do with developing courage. But, they don't know that a successful person can never be whole without this. That is why it is important to connect spiritually.

Below are the reasons why spirituality is needed to be courageous:

Spiritual Individuals Are Gracious. Psychology demonstrated that expressing gratitude is connected with numerous positive emotions like overall vitality, generosity with resources and time, and optimism. Spirituality also encourages everyone to be positive, expressed in various life practices.

Spiritual Individuals Are Compassionate. Experiencing compassion toward some people is one of the things that people from living with spiritual life. Various pro-social or positive emotions have strong links with spiritualism, like feeling great about some things in life.

Spiritual Individuals Flourish. Many said that spirituality is linked to numerous aspects of human-like life. Those who are spiritual have positive relationships, are optimistic, have high self-esteem, and have purpose and meaning in life.

Spiritual Individuals Self-Actualize. People who have a high level of spirituality strive to get a better life. They also consider fulfillment and personal growth as their central goal. Spirituality is also considered a path toward self-actualization. The reason behind it is that this requires everyone to focus on the internal values and work to be a better individual.

Spiritual Individuals Take Time for Savoring Life Experiences. People who value spirituality take time to reflect on their everyday activities and build lasting memories of their experiences. Since spiritual individuals are more conscious about their activities learn to be content from the small pleasures in life.

Being spiritual may be hard for some people. However, if you want to face this crazy world, you need courage and spirituality to succeed.

HAPPINESS STARTS WITH YOU

Introduction

We strive to achieve our objectives and goals throughout our lives. We believe that if we reach prosperity, we will be content and at peace with the world. This might be the case. However, it is a basic reality that not everyone will be successful. Only a small percentage of the population will rise to the peak of riches and power. The majority of us are doomed to live mediocre lives.

So, does this indicate that only a tiny number of individuals will be happy in their lives? Is it true that only the wealthy, powerful, and successful have the right to be happy?

Fortunately, the answer is no. If you want to live a happy and meaningful life, you don't need much money or power. Happiness, after all, is a mental condition.

It doesn't matter if you have all of the money in the world. Even if you did, you might not be happy. But on the other hand, you can be happy even if you don't have many things.

In this in-depth guide to happiness, you'll discover that your happiness is unrelated to your financial situation, job, or social position. It all begins with you.

CHAPTER 1: THE ROAD TO HAPPINESS

Simple things can bring the most happiness. In this case, Izabella Scorupco is. Various qualities make us happy. Is your happiness the same as someone else's?

If you don't like what other people call what makes them happy and fulfilled, you might not like them.

Maintaining a decent family and being healthy might make people happy. For some people, it might be their jobs and careers that are important to them. For some people, it's their money and how well they're known in the community. A lot of people enjoy good food and drinks more than anything else. The list keeps going.

With that said, researchers have been arguing for a long time about what happiness is. Why? There are too many things that can make someone happy or unhappy. It's agreed that "happiness is the state of being happy."

Many people don't agree with this definition of happiness, but I think it's important to understand what happiness is. It's a mental state that shows how you feel daily. It shows how you think about your life, such as whether you're happy or not happy with how your life is going. If you're not happy, then it's clear that you aren't satisfied. Isn't it great if you're?

The thing is, just because someone is happy doesn't mean they won't feel bad. Nothing is truer than this. Happy people still have problems and trials, but they deal with them differently than people who are unhappy would. It's what makes them different from everyone else.

Those who are happy aren't afraid to try new things. They're less likely to have bad feelings. People don't walk all over them. Their happiness makes people want to be around them. We know someone is happy when we see them. It looks better with them there.

It doesn't matter what we think happiness is. We all need more of it in our lives, no matter what. If everyone on this planet is happy, the world will be a much better place to live in.

CHAPTER 2: FIGURE OUT WHY YOU'RE UNHAPPY

To be unhappy, we have to not know what we want and then kill ourselves to get it. - Don Herold, too.

When you're always blue and can't remember when you were happy and free, you need to figure out why as soon as possible. It's not good for anyone to stay in a bad mood because it can quickly become depression. There is still time to help. If you want to figure out what's making you unhappy, here are a few questions to ask yourself.

No, I'm not doing what I want to be doing now.

Ask yourself this important question. Was there something I could do? No, I'm not taking any steps to get the job or job I want. Is your day job one that you don't enjoy, but it pays the bills?

For a lot of people, this is a problem. They know they don't like their jobs, but they stay in them year after year. If they don't like it, they may think they have no other choice. Over time, their jobs become a place where they feel safe. They start to be afraid of following their dreams. Then, if you're one of them, you should figure out how you can free yourself to do what you want and love in life.

Before, you might have had little say in the matter. Likely, your parents didn't support your dream of becoming a musician, a professional athlete, or a good artist. They've probably heard stories about people who went after their dreams and ended up hungry and homeless. To not break your parents' rules, you do what they say even though you don't want to. You work at a job you hate.

You should act now if this story sounds familiar or if you're still in the same place. Can't you find anything? People who do what they love The steps you are taking to get out of this trap are:

Answers: I hope that your answers will help you see the light, so you can finally start looking for a job that makes you happy.

Yes, my thoughts are making me unhappy.

You can decide what kind of thoughts you want to think about. You can choose to think positively, or you can choose to think the other way around. In this case, you're going to be unhappy.

If you don't want to think about bad things, you can tell yourself to stop. I know this is easier said than done, but it's true. We can bump our heads as much as we want, but the negative thoughts will stay in the background. This is why some people go crazy. When they listen to the noises, it doesn't matter what they do. They can't stop hearing them

Visualization is very important when you want to get rid of negative thoughts. You also need to be self-aware and pay attention to your ideas.

Right now, there's a trick you can try: Every time your mind starts to think bad, tell yourself to stop. Take a deep breath and imagine that your whole body is covered in oil and that the negativity is sliding off of you as you breathe in and out. There will be less negativity in your mind when you get rid of it.

You want to be the best you can be.

It isn't one of the things you should be aiming for. Why? The reason why is because when you set a model as your goal, you're inevitably setting yourself up to fail. Even worse, if you give it, you're the only one who will be disappointed, and that's not good.

Aim for something more realistic than perfection, like being good at what you do. It's still a big deal, but at least it's easier to reach now. No one is best, so why do we try to be perfect?

Perfection is, to put it simply, not worth it. When you want to be perfect, you set the bar so high that even a small mistake can make everything you've worked for fall apart.

However, if you want to be the best, you give yourself a chance to succeed. You won't be afraid to go.

Because you know your chances of making it are good, go out and make a fool of yourself. You use your mistakes and failures as ways to learn.

And what's the other good thing about aiming for excellence? You'll always have room to grow. It doesn't matter if you are the best at your job, school, or sport. You can still do even better the next time.

Once you figure out why you're unhappy, you'll be able to move forward and finally be on the path to happiness.

CHAPTER 3: BE GRATEFUL AND BE APPRECIATIVE

" Time and health are two valuable things that we don't value until they are gone. " As he says, "Denis Waitley."

When your unhappiness eats away at your soul, and you think everything you have is going to waste, think again. You might be wrong. Look around. What do you think? What are you smelling? What are you hearing? Look up at the sky now. Looked at it? No, I don't like the sound of leaves moving in the wind. Or the way the grass feels on your feet?

What would happen if you lost everything? Imagine not being able to see, hear, touch, or smell. Your sense of taste and your sense of smell. Take a moment to think about what you're not getting.

Imagine not being able to feel, hear, or see for the rest of your life. It's very hard, isn't it? Life as we know it is over. You might want to end your own life right now.

Because your life won't be the same ever again,

Fortunately, the above is just a game. A powerful one, too. I hope it made you realize how small your problems are compared to having everything taken away from you. This is what happened to me.

You should be grateful for these ten things:

1. Life.

Every time you wake up, you get another chance at life. Make up for what you've done in the past and start a new life. Make a difference in this world. Currently reside each day as if that was your last. This will be the best day of your life!

2. Family.

Connect with people no matter how busy life gets.

Your family. They gave you life. If you don't have them, you will be nothing. The same goes for if you have siblings. Learn to love them as well. If you have a large family, spend time with them as well. People in your family helped you become who you are today.

3. Friendship.

A good friend is important. In this case, there is someone you can talk to about your thoughts and feelings. You don't have to be alone because of this. They can help you have a better life, and you can help them have a better one, too. Have meaningful talks with your friends.

4. Health.

Good health isn't always given the attention it deserves. Take care of your body. When we get sick, we're only reminded to be grateful for our health. Even the smallest pain can bother us a lot, and more so if it's a serious or critical illness.

5. Love.

It doesn't matter if you're in love with someone romantically or platonically, for yourself or someone else. It is full of wisdom to say that "love makes the world go around." Having a good time makes you feel alive. It makes you want to get out of bed early, walk with a spring in your step, smile and laugh more, and do many other good things.

6. Laughter.

No matter how bad your life is, there's always something to laugh about. Laughter has a lot of good things going for it, like making you healthier. When you laugh, you lower your level of stress. As soon as you have a good laugh with someone else, the two of you start to feel like you know each other better.

7. Tears.

If you cry, people might think you're being mean. But tears aren't all that bad! Sometimes, tears are good. It helps to see things differently. There is a lot more value in life and laughter now.

8. Nature.

There is less nature now than there was a few million years ago, but there is still a lot to enjoy. As even if you live in a big city, you can still take a look around. Plants and trees bring a lot of greenery to the world.

Animals graze on the grass. Watch and be amazed at how nature takes back what she owns from places that have been left behind.

9. Time.

The amount of time we have is not unlimited. When we're born, our bodies start to figure out how long we have left. So, we can't let small problems in our lives get us down.

Down. Let's make the most of the short time we have here on Earth.

10. Yourself.

Yes, I am right. Learn to love yourself. You aren't perfect, and no one is because no one is. When your mother gave birth to you, you were very small. You've grown a lot since then. What have you done, and what have you failed at? What do you hope for, and what do you dream of? Now think about the people you've met and how you've helped them. Think about what you're going to leave behind when you die.

Learn to be grateful for both the good and bad things in your life. Everything comes together to give you a unique life experience that's meant to push you and bring out your best self. When you stop worrying about everything and start appreciating the small things in life, your happiness will show up not just to you but to everyone else, too.

CHAPTER 4: EMBRACE AND WELCOME CHANGE

If we wait for another user or another time, change will not happen. All along, we have been waiting for you, and we are finally here. We are the change we want.

This is a quote from a man named Barack Obama:

Is that true? Then, do what you need to do so that you can be pleased! Simple as that. But, of course, life isn't always that simple. To say you'll change is so much easier than to do it.

When things change for the better or worse, there are two types of things that happen: Often, it isn't clear at first whether the change you're making will be good or bad. You have to take a risk and do something more often than not.

When it comes to change, you can start it or wait for it to happen. The nice thing was if you began it, you could take more control of it than if you only reacted to it. Even though the change is coming, this also helps the user deal with it because you know it will. You won't feel like this came out of nowhere hit you.

The transformation was seen as bad by individuals who don't like it, but there are many good reasons to welcome change. Several of them:

- **You can find new ways to make money.**

There are true changes all over the place. When you're ready to accept change, it's easier for you to find opportunities that are hidden. Besides, some people might say that the chance will come to you. This is because when you accept change, you also open your eyes. When someone else is running away from the change, you're walking right into it with your eyes wide open. There is a better chance of seeing new opportunities because of this.

- **You'll become a better person.**

If you don't like change, you're going to keep doing the same things over and over again. For real, there's no space for anyone else in this room.

Grow and improve as a person. It's possible to change your bad habits and start new ones. When you move from one place to another, you get a bigger view of the world. There are things you learn and things you adapt to when you move. The only way to move forward is to welcome change with open arms.

- **You'll learn about your strengths (and weaknesses)**

To find out your strengths and flaws, you need to accept and embrace change. When you get a new job, many things can happen. The dream hire might turn out to be good than the old one, but instead, your performance will soar. Also, if you start a new business right away, you'll find out what you're good at and what you should outsource.

As time goes on, you'll learn new ways to solve problems.

When you don't fight change, you'll develop new ways to solve problems. Seeing new places makes you think outside the box. People who are open to new things can be more creative when they change things up. It lets you look for new solutions more quickly and effectively. But if you didn't accept change in the first place, you'd be stuck with the same old problems.

Accepting change is a part of living a happy life. It means leaving your comfort zone. Ask yourself, what can you do right now that will make you happy?

No, I don't need to change jobs. No, I don't think so. Does moving to another city or even another country makes you happy? Only you can answer this question.

Remember that if you want to be truly happy, you should look for and embrace change.

CHAPTER 5: SAY GOODBYE TO YOUR BAD HABITS

To get rid of negative habits, they come from good ones. Jerome says:

To be happy, you need to get rid of your nasty habits and start making good ones. It's not easy to do this. It's because bad habits take a long time to form. This is why. It doesn't happen quickly. Instead, it occurs over time until you make the habit out of habit. Think about it, but don't. You do it. Then, you know you've made a habit.

Bad habits make you unhappy in the long run, which is not a good thing. There is a good chance that you will feel good about yourself while you're doing the routine or habit. But it won't be good for you or your health as time goes on.

Smoking is one example. When you smoke, you feel better. Taking a puff of cigarette smoke helps you lower your stress level to manageable. But on the other hand, smoking can have many adverse effects on your health. There are many long-term effects of smoking. These include brain damage, emphysema, tooth decay, and so much more. Even the people who breathe in your second-hand smoke are at risk of getting these diseases. On the other hand, smoking is only going to give you short-term pleasure. People die in the long run.

Breaking bad habits will also take some time, but it won't be quick. You'd have to work on it and be able to tell when you're making the habit. People need self-control and discipline to be able to stop it, so they need those things to do so

Use these tips to help you stop your bad habits:

What are the things that make you want to do something?

There are three parts: a trigger (or cue), a routine (or task), and then the reward. There could be many things that could make someone want to smoke, such as eating. People often want to smoke after they've eaten. Or, it could be that stress is what makes you angry. Stress makes you want to smoke more.

It's important to know what your cues or triggers are before you can break a bad habit. Study your bad habits and think about why you do them. If you want to stop drinking alcohol, don't buy alcohol. Feel free to tell friends that you're trying to stop when you're out with them. People who care about you won't drink with you if you have good friends. If your relatives are still pressuring you to drink, you might want to spend less time with them and look for more supportive people.

Cut down on your stress.

When we have a lot of stress in our lives, bad habits can start to form. When you're stressed, you begin to smoke. You start drinking when you're too tired or have problems at home, so you start drinking more. When you have a lot of work to do, you begin to procrastinate, and you begin to do it. There are times when you need a mental pick-me-up. You drink a lot of coffee to help you do this. Here's how you do it.

Some people have bad habits when they are stressed. These are just a few. If you find that you're reacting negatively to stress, then it's time to do something. How? By doing everything you can to lessen your stress levels.

Try to find a way to avoid situations that make you stressed, so your stress levels will decrease. It's usually impossible to live a stress-free life, so you need to face it head-on and learn how to control or deal with stress.

It's important to note that stress isn't always bad. They say that even some pressure is excellent for us. When we eat food, it makes us want to live. It helps us do our jobs faster and better. Getting stressed out all the time is only wrong when you let it take over your life.

When you start a bad habit, link it to a new and better one.

To change a bad habit and start a better one, you can use an "anchor" system. This is a simple way to do this. How it works: Every time you start to make a bad habit, you do the new one instead. This is how it works:

A bad habit like biting your nails might be one you want to change, for example. Suppose this lousy habit is caused by stress. Now, you also want to read or listen to inspirational content to help you grow as a person.

A good book is always close by, so you read a few pages when you bite your nails. Or you can go to YouTube and listen to the motivational speakers you like the most. Nail-biting will be off your list of bad habits after doing this routine for a few weeks.

List all the reasons you should stop the habit, and then decide if you should do it.

There's a good reason terrible habits are called "bad." They have adverse effects that may or may not show up right away. For example, you can drink. You know that when you drink too much, you get a terrible hangover in the morning. When you were out in public, you're likely to have thrown up a few times. Some of your friends might not invite you to social events or parties anymore because they're afraid you will drink too much and make a mess.

Write down all the things that will happen if you keep drinking and use that as your "why." When you write your descriptions, try to make them as detailed and detailed as possible. Make a move every time.

Make a mistake and go back to your old ways. Check this list and promise to do better next time.

Keep an eye on yourself and see if there are any bad habits that you need to break. Even if you turn your life around and live a happy life, you may pick up some new bad habits down the road.

That's fine. Everyone is not the same, and no one is perfect. Just pick up where you left off and keep working on becoming a better person every single day.

CHAPTER 6: LEARN TO LOVE YOURSELF FIRST

It's not fair to let someone else lower your self-esteem because that's what it is. You must first love yourself before anyone else can love you. In this case, Winnie Harlow is the person who said this.

First, you need to love yourself. If you want to be sincerely happy and fulfilled with the entire planet, you need to love yourself. Unless you love yourself first, you can't entirely love someone else.

Is it easy to tell if you love yourself enough? Tips:

Your mirror is your best friend.

A beautiful or handsome face doesn't make you look good. You don't even need one of the most stunning faces in the whole world to enjoy your looks. You also don't need to have a body like a supermodel to say you look good. We can't all be so lucky to win the lottery of genes. But, the truth is, even people we think look "perfect" have their insecurities, as well.

Trying to make ourselves look perfect is the only way to enjoy what we see when we look in the mirror. This is false. Is it going to stop? If we always compare ourselves to others and look for flaws even when there aren't, will it? Forget about being happy with your looks or yourself. You'll do have something to say about it.

The cosmetic technique has indeed made great strides over the last few years. If you want to look the way you want to, you can now do so. But at what cost? It is not free to get cosmetic surgery. This means that you should expect to pay a lot of money to have it done. They can't look in the mirror because they don't have that much money. But, do you need to? Encouraging news: You should not have to.

To be willing to accept yourself as you are, even if your appearances aren't perfect, operate on that—no matter whether or not you like it. I was born with this face. You can look at the world that can't be seen as soon as you can.

Once you get used to your own body, the mirror will become your best friend.

You put yourself first and everyone else second.

No, being selfish is not the same as putting yourself first. It just means you love yourself more than other people. It's different, though, if you go to the extreme, that is, step over other people to get what you want. But, if you don't hurt anyone, then it's OK.

A big problem with most people is that they don't want to hurt someone else's feelings. They do what their parents want and what their spouse wants. They quickly give in to the pressure of their peers, even though they know what they're being asked to do goes against their morals.

Giving in to people you like and love is OK, but don't do it all the time. Could you not make it a habit? It's straightforward for your "friends" to take advantage of your trust. Unless you learn to stand up for yourself and fight for what you believe in, they can quickly get you to do what they want.

It is not a sign of selflessness if you let other people walk on top of you. I think it shows that you're not very smart, for lack of a better term. You are a living person. It's your dreams, goals, and life. Don't waste your time making other people happy if you're not satisfied.

Aren't happy at first. To make everyone happy, you first need to love yourself fully.

You look after your body and your health.

When you let your health go to waste, it says that you don't like yourself very much. In the adage, "Your body is your temple," you are correct: In other words, if you don't take care of your body, then you're not taking care of your temple.

You don't need to join a gym right now. No, you don't have to buy all organic food from here on out. You can take good care of your health by paying attention to your body and what it needs. Make healthy food a habit and stop giving yourself junk food. Stop doing anything wrong for your body. It's not cool to do things like smoke, drink, or take drugs. In the short term, these may make you happy. In the long run, you're going to have a hard time.

Listen to your body. Sleep when you're stressed and tired. Take a day to rest. Make plans to go away for a few days over the weekend. Sometimes, you may also want to do nothing all day. If you watch Netflix all at once all the time, it's not the best thing to do. It might not be a big deal if they go every week or every month.

It's even better if it helps you forget about stressful things like work.

Give yourself space to breathe. All work and no play make Jack a dull boy. To have fun, you also give your body a break from the stress and strain of your daily life by going on a trip.

CHAPTER 7: BUILD POSITIVE RELATIONSHIPS

"Praise your relationships, not your things." In this case, Anthony J. D'Angelo is the person who wrote the text:

Material things can make you happy, but not almost as much if you share them with people you care about and love. After all, we are wired to thrive when we contact other people and make friends.

People in your family instantly connected to you when you were born. This includes your parents, siblings, and anyone else in your family. At school, you had friends. When you went off to work, you had friends and coworkers there to help you out. Then, too. You are going to go.

You'll make and keep friends with many people throughout your whole life.

As it is, not all relationships will be good and happy. You're likely to have a lot of bad relationships with people in your life, including your closest family and friends.

To be happy, you need to spend less and less time with people who aren't nice. To get rid of them, you should try. Because living your life without them might be challenging, but if it's the best thing for you, then do it. Sometimes, all you need is a clean break to move your happiness meter from empty to full.

In the right company, your happiness will be off the charts. There are a lot of better things that will happen for you. The best part of your day or even your whole month is going to be spending time with good people. If you don't spend enough time with them, it could even be the highlight of your whole year.

Here are a few ways to start building good relationships with the people in your life:

Get to know people.

The shy type should start getting out of their shells. Take the lead and start talking to people now. Say something nice and try to build trust, and then see if you can start a conversation. Some people might want to be alone. But for most people, when someone else starts the conversation, they come out of their shell, too. Enjoy meeting a new person!

Be a little kinder.

Even if you don't like it, being more understanding is one of the best ways to build relationships with other people. Try to be more open-minded when you meet new people, so you can get to know them better. After all, we are all different. We are all unique people with our thoughts, feelings, and cultures. Imagine yourself in the other person's shoes to figure out where they're coming from when you are more understanding.

Be a good person to listen to.

When you listen to someone, you do more than just act as their sounding board. You should pay attention to what the person is saying and try to figure out what they're saying, not just nod and say "yes."

Absentmindedly. You can be a good friend if you listen well. It shows that you care about the other person.

Be a good person to talk to.

For communication to work smoothly, it is important to keep lines of communication open and clear. This is why it's important to work on your communication skills. If you think everyone else understands what you're saying, but they're taking it the wrong way, it's very easy to think that way.

Many things can make relationships go bad because of this. You're saying one thing, but the other user is hearing it in a very different way.

A good relationship can do so much for us. The more positive relationships you have, the happier you will be on a general level. The spouse that makes us feel good about ourselves helps us go through the motions of life in a better mood. This, in turn, makes you enjoy life more, which is a good thing.

CHAPTER 8: THE RIGHT CHOICES IN LIFE

"Our lives are the sum of all the decisions we have made in the past." He said that Wayne Dyer was a great person.

We make decisions all day long. Most don't require a lot of thought; you just know what you're going to do. When it comes to many things, you need to stop and think about your decision for a while. You need to think about the pros and cons of all the options you have. Choosing the right thing to do when the stakes are high, and you could lose something important is very important.

Lost is never fun, especially when you have to give up something important. For example, if you make a bad choice, your job and relationships could be at risk, as well as your happiness and even your life.

In some decisions, you know right away what the outcome will be. It's clear-cut, right? To show how it works, you might be having trouble making up your mind if you're going to go to work this morning. To go or not to go? You're going to be paid. If not, then you won't get paid.

However, you won't know what will happen until a certain amount of time has passed for some decisions. For example, you've helped your friend start a business. For now, you know that your friend is good at business, but you won't know for months or even years whether you made the right choice.

How do you know if you're making the right choice in life? Three things to look for:

I think it's the right thing to do

Deep down, you know you're doing the right thing, even though your mind tells you you're making a mistake. You were right! Most of the time, you probably didn't even know why you did what you did.

That was the right thing to do. You know in your heart that it was the right choice.

Some people believe that your guardian angel or some other kind of power told you what to do. It's different for people who believe in science. They say it's a mix of past experiences and knowledge. Our brains figure out how to connect the dots and what to do with the information.

When people listen to their intuition and live to tell the tale, there are a lot of them. They've somehow been able to avoid accidents, disasters, bankruptcies, and other events that could change or end their lives. Try listening to what your gut tells you if you're having a hard time making a choice right now.

You're happy with the way you made your choice.

If you can live with your decision, it's a good sign that you made the right one. If you're going to be ashamed of it, then it's the wrong one. People can be attracted to someone even though they're already married, and this person has also told you that they feel the same way about you. This is a good example of how this works.

Should you keep going with the relationship or not? If you can live with the thought of ruining someone else's marriage, then that's up to you. Then, but if

So, if you think it is wrong, you should do the right thing. In the end, you'll be happy with yourself. You can sleep well at night because you know you didn't cheat and break up your marriage.

You've thought about the pros and cons.

Big decisions need to be looked at. If you listen to your gut instinct in some situations, you probably won't get any help from it at all. For example, moving to a new country is not a small thing. Leaving everything you know behind isn't going to be easy. But you know that there's a better chance for you somewhere else.

Your gut instinct is likely to tell you to stay, but your logic might tell you to go for it, as well. The pros and cons of each choice should be written down. Then take a few days to think about it and come back to it when you've thought things through.

As long as you go after what makes you happy, everything else doesn't matter As you think about what you want to do, you can ask for advice from other people. But remember that it's your life, and your actions will have a bigger impact on you than on anyone else.

LIFE HACK: CREATING A
BETTER YOU

The S twins: Success and Self-Improvement

Every part of your story has a reason for being there. In your life, there are both highs and lows. There may be an instinct, though, to hide in a cave, lock the door, and cry a river about things that happened in the past. Key: Use that as a step and platform for your growth and success. That's what you need to do.

How does one get to the bridge? By taking these steps:

1) You must change your mindset: You must be your own biggest fan! Make it past the point where you're going to fail and into success. Be happy with every step.

2) Setting goals is the second thing you should do. Make them small and easy to reach.

3) Competition: Look inside and not outside. See yourself, not other people, as your main competitor.

4) Learn: Look at everything as a chance to learn. Learn all the time! Everything is an opportunity for you to get something out of it, so look at it that way.

Feel good: Smiling has been shown to make people feel better. Smile a lot more now.

Have people around you who you want to be like. Everybody who is around you makes up for you.

Why?

It will always be you who is your main rival in the race of life! The big problem is that many people look at the next lane and think that the person there is better than them.

It's somehow better. Because if you were to sit down with them and talk about their story, you most likely would prefer your version over theirs. In the mirror, take a moment to enjoy what you see.

You are a mother having a hard time with your tantrum-throwing child. There is an oversized hoodie and a pair of jeans on you on Saturday morning, which is your best outfit. When you go shopping, you want to stop the child from picking up everything in the store. When a pretty woman in a crop top with washboard abs walks by, you are on the phone. When she walks around, you just want to. She's thinking, "I'm tired of this life. I wish I had a family at home to come back to," but you may not know that. The woman may even have had a few miscarriages, but she just wants to have a child.

We say, "Wooh... he's got it." His first thought in the morning is, "I need to go to AA classes. I can't do this on my own!"

Funny, right? We get jealous when we see how good other people are, but things are still not perfect, even in that perfect state. Our low self-esteem and self-confidence make us make a web of dark despair.

I know a person who talks all the time. People don't pay attention to what she says most of the time. She doesn't listen or give anyone a chance to say anything. People didn't want to be in circles in the past when she was around.

Getting what you want doesn't happen on its own. When someone has a good story, there is a long journey with many ditches and bridges. Allow the journey to begin. When you start to learn and improve, the lessons start. The world is your classroom. Class is in progress.

One way to improve yourself is to find a wise person to talk to. Someone who you can trust and open up to. Find someone willing to tell you more than just what you want to hear. Arrogant: Do you think I'm a little bit of a jerk? Do I always talk too much? Do I talk too loud? Do you think my breath smells? Be honest and open with the person. As well, let your mind and heart open up so that you can accept any constructive criticism that comes your way.

This is very important because it will help you become better.

The fastest way to stop growth is to compare things. Love and respect who you are now. You can't go anywhere until you start.

When a spouse wants to help the other person improve their self-esteem, they should not criticize them. Starting, you should love and accept that person. By making them feel safe and loved, you let them trust and feel like they belong. That act of love will be the main thing that makes them want to improve their own lives.

Improve your life and learn how to love yourself without having to stand on top of a mountain and say you're great. It's the virtue of being able to accept and be content. When we improve ourselves, we start to feel good, content, and happy.

The process of building a better you.

So, how can you stay calm, composed, and have high self-esteem in a bad situation? Here are some things you might want to think about as you start to improve yourself.

In your thought, think of yourself as a Dart Board. You can think of everything and everyone around you as Dart Pins. They hurt you in so many ways when they hit you. Now, how can you stop them from coming?

This is Dart Pin #1.

Keep an eye out for the "survival of the fittest theory" that can happen in a bad work environment. Some places don't encourage people to work together but instead, turn into a war zone. Getting into a fight that never ends is easy. "Stop!" The more you do this, the less confident you will be, so stay away from it. See other people at work as a way to learn. What can you learn from other people's stories?

Dart Pin #2: The way other people act

There is nothing you can do about how other people act. You can only amend how you react to how they act. Everyone else is not in charge of you. In this case, don't worry about what other people do. Instead, worry about what you do.

It's Dart Pin #3:

Change is hard. People don't know what to do in this new place. It reveals our flaws. Gold is changed by fire. It grows, but in the end, it ends up in shape it was meant to be. In the short term, change may make you feel bad. This is a chance for you to improve yourself. There are many things you need to do at your new job. In time, as you know how to ride the significant changes, they will lift you.

It's Dart Pin # 4.

The past hurts but doesn't stay there—a chance to learn and a point to remember. The pity party will eat you if you stay too long.

Dart Pin #5: How we think

How each person sees things will make them unique. The world is filled with bad things. Do not get caught up in them. Every time you find yourself in a dark place, try to find the light even if you have to be the light!

Determination Theory is the sixth pin on the dartboard.

What makes you who and what you are is a mix of genetics and the way you live. Remember that you don't have to follow the bad habits that your family has. As long as someone's parent was an alcoholic, you can make doubly sure you don't fall down the same hole.

Isn't life a choice-based thing? The choice is yours. Having affirmations when you wake up every day can help you have a good day. This will help you decide how your day goes. Choose to speak positive words, and decide that it will not change your stand even if someone says something bad. There will be more and more of that as you do it. The choice is yours today. You can choose to build your self-esteem or not. There isn't a magic genie in this story. "Michael, I have given you the order to now improve your life." God wouldn't come down from heaven and say that.

Let's face it: This is true. In a bad situation, life can be very hard. Think of life as a fight. Several wars must be won. Remember to wear the right armor to protect you from random attacks. When you fall, don't forget that it doesn't mean you've lost the war or battle. Once you get up, you can fight again. The more you fight, the tougher you get, and the stronger you get, too! That's how it works when you want to improve yourself.

Take the blame for your shortcomings. You can't start to improve yourself if you don't admit that something is wrong. What's interesting is that as you fight, you move up the ranks in the military, which is interesting. As time goes on, you become the leader of the team. Then you become the person people go to when they need help with their self-esteem. You become part of a group. Because I have been there, I know.

Where Is Your Faith?

I need God, and so do you, right?

People who want to grow spiritually have to fight against the temptations of money, power, and crazy things. Technology also plays a big part by giving us easy, fancy gadgets that have taken our minds off what's important and made them more fun. We lose sight of how important we are and how important we are to other people. We can find a balance between the material and spiritual parts of our lives in many ways.

To grow spiritually, you have to look inside.

The things you think, believe and do. It is important to learn how to be introspective and look inside yourself. Flow with the flow of your mind. Ask that you do what you do. Learn how to keep every thought in your head. Every decision you make should be looked at again, and you should learn to look inside for perspective and great ideas about your life goals. It's time to let go of things that are bad or questionable. As soon as you are truly honest, you will be able to know and accept your flaws, as well as toss them. Practice, but also be willing and brave to look inside and find the truths that are inside of you. Forgive yourself for any negative thoughts or actions you may have had or done. Then, move on to the next thing!

To grow spiritually is to use your abilities to the fullest.

Religion and science have different ideas about how the human spirit works. Religion sees people as spiritual beings who are only here on Earth for a short time. Science sees the spirit as just one part of an individual. It's a common theme in both Western and Eastern religious ideas. It is important to put the body's needs in front of the spirit's needs. Experiences, good deeds, and beliefs are the blueprint for the growth of a spiritual being. It's called self-actualization in Psychology when you reach your full potential and become the person you want to be.

Maslow came up with a list of human needs, including physiological, security, belongingness, esteem, cognitive, aesthetic, self-actualization, and self-transcendence. James had already broken down these three needs into the material, emotional, and spiritual. Spiritual or existential needs come next when you have taken care of your physical and emotional needs. Each need that is met leads to the total development of the person. If you look at Christianity and Islam, you might think that self-development is a way to serve God. On the other hand, psychology thinks that self-development should be an end in and of itself.

To grow spiritually, you have to look for a reason.

There are a lot of religions out there that believe in God, like Christianity and Judaism. They think that the goal of life is to serve the creator of all things. Several theories in psychology say that we give meaning to our lives in the end. To grow in spirit, whether we believe that life's meaning is pre-planned or up to us, we need to know that we don't just exist. We don't know what our lives are all about when we are born. The way we learn about ourselves and the world we live in isn't always the same. We interact with other people and act and react to our situations. There are some beliefs and values that we don't agree with, and there are some that we do. Our lives have a reason. When things get tough, this purpose keeps us going. It also gives us something to look forward to, like a goal or a destination we're working toward. A person who doesn't have a goal or a reason is like a ship drifting at sea.

To grow spiritually, it's important to see how things are connected.

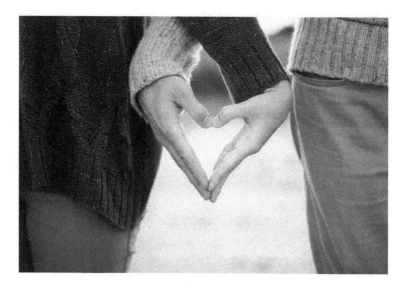

Religions emphasize the idea that we are connected to everything in the world, both living and nonliving. It doesn't matter if there aren't any blood relatives between two people who call each other "brother and sister." Christianity and Islam, for example, talk about the relationship between humans and higher power in their religious texts. On the other hand, scientists talk about how we're related to other living things through the idea of evolution. This connection can be seen in the idea of ecology, which is the way living and nonliving things work together. In psychology, connectedness is a feature of self-transcendence, which Maslow says is the most important human need. Making the connection between everything makes you more humble and respectful of people, animals, plants, and other things in the world, as well as your connection to them. There is a lot more to look at and enjoy. To be a productive member of everyone around you, you have to get out of your way.

To grow in spirit, we have to face it every day. We win some, we lose some, but the most important thing is that we learn, and from this knowledge, we can grow even more in our faith.

What is your source of strength?

What makes you feel good? Pain can be good for some people because it makes them want to change. Bad grades can show us that we need to study. Having debts may make someone want to start their own business. Making us feel like we're not good enough is what gives us the "push" to speak up and fight for ourselves so that we don't do it again. Whether it's something we've done that was bad, a friend's sad story, the best movie ever, or a book that makes us want to improve ourselves, these things can help us get up and be motivated to do better.

How can you stay on track with all the bad things that happen globally? Make sure you try the tips. They are called the ABCs of life.

The first step is to A. Take a stance. Avoid bad people, things, and places. In the past, Eleanor Roosevelt said that "the future belongs to those who believe in the beauty of their dreams."

B. It is important to believe in your abilities and what you can do.

C. Look at things from every angle and perspective. Motivation comes from a strong desire. To understand life, you need to feel the sun from both sides.

D. Don't give up and don't give in. Once, twice, and more than three times, Thomas Edison tried to develop a new idea and make a light bulb that worked well. Make motivation the wheel of your car.

E. Enjoy yourself. As if you don't need money, work hard. Dance as if no one is looking. As if you had never cried. In other words, learn as if you'll live forever. When people are happy, they get more excited.

F. Family and Friends are life's most important "F" things. Keep an eye on them.

G. Give more than you think is enough. When people are motivated and want to improve their own lives, it happens at work, but where? In the house? During class? When you put in extra effort when you do things.

H. Keep your dreams alive. In the beginning, they might hang out there for a while. But these little stars will be the thing that makes you go!

I. People who try to hurt you should not bother you. Don't let other people get you down. You don't want to be friends with people who aren't happy when you do well. They don't want to hear about it.

J. Be yourself. Being yourself is the most effective approach to advance. Make matters worse by attempting to please everyone.

K. As hard as life may seem right now, don't give up, even if it's not easy. When motivated, he sees a rough life start to get easier, making it easier for him to improve himself.

L. Love yourself. Now, isn't that simple?

M. People make things happen. What makes you want to do something is to put your dreams into work clothes.

N. Don't lie, cheat, or steal. Always play fair.

O. You should look around. People should learn how to act like a horse and read a horse. In two ways, they see things. One is how they want things to be, and the other is how things should be.

P. Practicing makes you better. Motivation is the key to practice. In this way, we can learn a wide range of skills and deal with our mistakes.

Q. People who give up don't win. Those who win don't give up, So, do you want to give up? or the winner?

R. Prepare yourself. Motivation isn't just about getting ready. Hear from the little voice inside of us before other people get up and push us around and try to move us. When Noah built the ark, it didn't rain.

S. Don't put things off.

T. Take charge of your own life now. A person who is disciplined or self-controlled also has a lot of drive. Both are important to self-improvement.

U. You should try to understand other people. You must be able to listen as well as speak. You should first want to learn and then want to be learned.

V. Make a picture. It's like putting a boat on dry land and not having a plan for it.

W. Wants it more than anything. Dreaming means believing. To believe is also something that comes from the roots of motivation and self-improvement, and it is something that comes from that.

X. X-Factor is what will make you stand out from the rest of the people around you. "Extras" can be things like more time for family, more help at work for your friends, and so on. When you're excited, you tend to add these things to your life.

Y: You are different from everyone else. It's not like anyone else in the world looks, acts, or talks like you. Because you're only going to spend your life and existence once, be grateful for what you have.

Z. Zig-zag toward your dreams. Go for it!

You can find the keys here.

To see what's in a painting, we have to look at it from a distance. It's hard to see what's deep underground if the painting is indeed an inch away from our face. That's not all. If we try to go a little farther, we'll be prepared to see the whole thing better.

We all desire to make a difference at some time in our lives. We also want to learn many things to help us become better people. Until then, we might not see something right in front of us. Only when things get bad do we think about unlocking our power to improve ourselves.

Suppose you want to know how to be a frog.

A: Try putting Frog A in a pot of hot water. What does happen now? He twirls around! He leaps off! Why? Because he can't deal with a sudden change in his environment, like the temperature of the water. Frog B: Immerse him in lukewarm water, then switch on the gas stove as well as wait. If you want to wait for the water to get hot, you can. "Oh... it feels a little hot in here." Frog B then thinks that.

Everybody is just like Frog B at the end of the day. Today, Katie thinks Jan doesn't like her very much. Tomorrow, Michael tells her that he doesn't like her. Anna doesn't care what her friends say about her, and she doesn't care what Anna thinks. The next day, she found out that Carrie and Mark didn't like her very much. Anna doesn't realize how important and necessary it is for her to improve herself until everyone in her community hates her.

When we hurt ourselves, we learn. Finally, we can see the signs and signals that things will get rough and tough as soon as we start to feel sick when none of our jeans or shirts fit us. At what time do we stop eating candy and chocolates? When we lose all of our teeth. In the beginning, it's hard to know that we need to stop smoking when our lungs aren't good.

We pray and ask for help all the time when we know that we're going to die tomorrow.

Usually, the only time most of us learn about unlocking our power to improve ourselves is when the world is falling apart. Because it's hard to change, we think and feel this way. It gets more painful when we don't pay attention to changes.

Like it or not, things will change. All of us will have different turning points in our lives. We will unlock our self-improvement power, not because the world says so, not because our friends are nagging us, but because we know it's for our good.

How would you describe someone happy? Now, you don't have to feel a lot of heat to know that you need to improve yourself. Your self-improvement ability comes from unlocking yourself from the thought that "it's just the way I am" so you can move forward. If you don't like change, this is a bad excuse. Most of us set up our minds like computers, and we do it all the time.

Jen tells everyone that she doesn't dare to be around people. She heard her mom, dad, sister, and teacher say the same things about her to other people all the time. Jen has always thought that way. She thinks it's her story. In other words: The first time there were many people at their house or school, she would hide in a room. Jen didn't just believe in her story; she lived it, too.

Her story says that Jen is the person she is in real life. Instead of having her story be plastered all over her face, she has to show people that "I'm important and I deserve to be treated that way!" This is how she should be treated.

Everybody might not like the word "self-improvement." If we look at things from a different perspective, we may be more inclined to appreciate the process rather than focus on how long it will take us to improve. Having three gym sessions a week, reading books instead of pornography, and going out with friends and peers will help you take a break from work. In the middle of the process of unlocking your self-improvement power, you'll start to see that you're becoming more relaxed and happy.

There are now...

Quick Course 7-Day Program to Improve Yourself.

There have been so many celebrity marriages that have broken up that I can't remember how many times I've read and heard about them. We often think of movie and TV stars as perfect people who live a life of wealth and glamour makes me wonder. I think we all have to stop putting our heads in the clouds and face the truth.

There are several other ways to lose your concept of self, even if the thing is small. But we should all try to remember who we are, no matter what.

How are you different from the rest? Think about something and continue improving on these things for one week.

There are many things you need to think about on

Day 1.

Are you looking for happiness, health, and money in your life, but you don't know where to start? If you know your life purpose or mission statement, you will have a unique compass that will always take you on the proper path to your truth.

Seeing yourself in a tight or even dead end may make this seem hard at first. Even though things can go wrong, there's always a way to change things. You can make a big difference to yourself.

Day 2: What do you believe in?

What do you care about the most? Make a list of the five things that are important to you. Some are security, freedom, family, spiritual growth, and learning. As you put down your goals for this year, make sure they align with what you believe in. Make sure the goal fits with any of your top five values. If not, you might want to think about changing it or reconsidering the goal itself.

The number shouldn't bother you, but it should make you want to do more than you ever thought possible.

This is Day 3. Find out more about who you are.

Needs that haven't been met can keep you from living a true life. Care for yourself. Do you want to be recognized, to be right, to be in charge, or to be loved? If so, you may need to work on this. Many people don't live their lives the way they want to, and most of them end up stressed or even depressed because of it. This is a list of your top 4 needs. Make sure they are met before it's too late!

Day 4: Find out what you like.

You consider who you are and how much you love doing in life... This is what you should do. Some things will only slow you down, but they won't stop you from becoming who you should be. Honor the people who have helped you become the person you want to be.

Day 5. Do what's best for you.

Reflecting in silence regularly can help you become more aware of your inner wisdom. Become one with nature. Breathe deeply to get your mind off of things. There aren't many places where city dwellers can even find the peace they want, even in their own homes. In my case, I like to just sit in a dark room and listen to classical music. The sound of music can help the savage beast be calm.

It's Day 6. Pay attention to what you can do well.

Describe what you like about yourself. What special skills do you have? Count three, and if you can't think of any, ask your friends and family for help. Are you creative, funny, and good with your hands? Find ways to show who you are through your strengths. When you can talk about what you know with other people, you can boost your self-confidence.

Day 7: Help other people.

If you live your life in a real way, you may find that you have a sense of being connected to other people. We all have a unique spirit or essence that we can share with others. When we live our purpose and share our talents with the world, we give back what we came to share with others in service to them. You get a lot of pleasure from sharing your gift with people close to you, but even more so if they see it through someone else's eyes.

Self-improvement is a type of work that is worth the time and money. It shouldn't always be inside an office building or even inside your room. The difference is in how much we want to change for the better.

As the book nears its end, I'd like to share with you some of my favorite quotes on how to improve yourself. I hope they help you!

One of the quotes: "Money is better than poverty, even if only for financial reasons." There is money involved, but it doesn't have to cost an arm and a leg to get it.

2. This is how it works: "That's what I think. The government is to blame "'That's enough.'

Then, 3 "Is there anything worse than death? Have you ever spent the night with a salesman from a company that sells insurance?" This is one of the most well-known ones. I mean, the thing about life's little problems isn't all that bad until "he" comes along. Maybe any author who writes about relationships will find out about this one day. Relationships can be complicated, but they can also be simple. If you're talking about the heart as in the heart that pumps blood through your body, we follow our hearts.

What do you think about sex? You can also continue to ask for more if you want more.

"That's just what you need to know about contraceptive pills: This is what you really ought to know. When I asked her to go to bed, she answered no." Sounds like a good idea. If he hits a nerve in everyday life, he doesn't have to sue.

6) "Basically, my wife was too young. Her coming into my bathroom would sink all of my boats." In the past, I didn't have a boat in my bathtub. While I'm taking a hot bath, just looking at it makes me sick.

When someone dies, "I don't want to be there." If it rains, it comes down.

In this case, "I am grateful for laughter, except when milk comes out of my nose." It could get even worse if you drink a lot of beer or mouthwash. It happened to me once.

Tell God about your ideas to make him laugh. Then, we're grateful for that. He doesn't hit us with lightning. What might happen in the next 10, 20, or 30 years doesn't matter. There are many ways to look at things, not just your own. The last time we didn't have any kind of wisdom that could help us was long ago. Religious or not, it doesn't matter if we get along or not when it comes to getting along. When you face your fears and learn how to deal with them, it takes more courage. So that's it.

Last but not least, here is the last piece of wisdom to remember... Any time, any place, and however we are

How to be happy: "Appreciate and enjoy what you have, rather than what you don't have."

LOVING YOUR IMPERFECT BODY

Bodies have an odor. They dribble. They sag, develop flaws, creak, and pain. They have hair growing from unexpected places, even when hair would not grow where it is desired. Bodies exist in different forms and sizes, all colors, and with various defects and abilities. And, as the children's book states, "everyone poops."

In summary, everybody has flaws and imperfections. Our bodies simultaneously hold our thoughts, dreams, and impulses while also helping us to see, hear, experience, and experience the world. While there may be a world beyond our physical selves, your body is the only home you have right now as a living, breathing human. It's critical to love your house, even if it has defects (which they all do)

Our body image affects our self-esteem, self-confidence, physical and mental health, and how we move through life. If you have trouble loving your body, keep reading to discover more about body image and how to improve it.

What Exactly Is Body Image

The phrase "body image" relates to how we feel about our bodies, how we physically occupy our bodies, and how we view ourselves - both mentally and in the mirror. Body image differs from appearance, and in many circumstances, our body image differs greatly from how an objective observer would characterize us

A Positive Self-Image

People who have a good body image are aware of their physical attractiveness. They understand that their physical appearance does not determine their worth as a person, and they are comfortable in their skin.

Having a positive body image does not imply that a person believes their body is flawless or without imperfections; rather, it implies that they recognize that everyone has flaws and is still worthy of love and respect.

A Poor Body Image

People who have a negative body image, on the other hand, are unable to accept their physical imperfections. A poor body image might result in emotions of shame or the desire to conceal. It can prevent people from participating in social activities and create barriers to closeness in relationships.

Individuals with low self-esteem may also spend excessive time and money "hiding" their flaws with cosmetics, accessories, or clothing, or seeking cosmetic procedures, only to find little relief from their appearance-related worry.

Individuals with a poor self-image may be concerned about perceived flaws that are not obvious or insignificant to an outside observer. In severe circumstances, a negative body may be present.

Physique dysmorphia occurs when a person perceives their body to be significantly different. A bodybuilder suffering from body dysmorphia, for example, may picture themselves in the mirror as a fragile, skinny wimp, even though they are objectively built like a tank.

A negative body image may lead to low self-esteem and self-confidence, and persons with a negative self-image are more prone to suffer from mental health problems such as depression and anxiety.

A poor body image is not the main cause of eating disorders, but it contributes. Even in those who do not have full-blown eating disorders, a poor body image can lead to disordered eating habits such as fasting, restricting food categories, dieting, binge, and excessive exercise, all of which can severely impact health and wellbeing

Concerned About Our Appearance

Unfortunately, today's culture encourages people to be self-conscious about their bodies. Even as North Americans get larger, our ideal body image becomes leaner — and more difficult to achieve. Fashion models, for example, used to be 8% smaller than the typical woman, but today they are 30% smaller — and several inches higher.

The physical ideal for guys has also evolved. Simply compare the starring guys in any Marvel film, with their carefully sculpted physique, to the biggest stars of the 1950s. Celebrities like James

Dean and Marlon Brando were certainly healthy and attractive. Still, they didn't spend hours in the gym or consume very precise diets under the constant supervision of trainers and nutritionists as today's incredibly thin and muscular stars do.

According to studies, both men and women are concerned about their looks. According to estimates, around 70% of women aged 18-30 dislike their bodies, and approximately 50% attempt to manage their weight through harmful practices. Forty-three percent of males dislike their bodies, increasing male body dissatisfaction.

A good body image is essential for living a happy, healthy, and well-adjusted life. A poor body image is harmful to our physical and emotional health, preventing us from accomplishing our goals. Start reading to learn more about how our body image develops during childhood and adolescence.

Body Image in Childhood and Adolescence

Our first task as babies is to figure out how our bodies operate. We can't even lift our heads at first, but soon we're crawling,

walking, and racing around, causing havoc. We begin to absorb information about which bodies are excellent and harmful as soon as we begin to learn to move our bodies. According to studies, youngsters as early as three years old may begin to worry about weight.

While people have always prized beauty - a stroll through any art museum will demonstrate this – today's worry about bodyweight is extremely severe, impacting youngsters earlier and younger. Girls began dieting at an average age of 14 in 1970, but by 1990, that age had reduced to 8. By the age of ten, more than 80% of girls had been on a diet.

In addition to being concerned about their weight, young toddlers begin to criticize others based on their weight. Obese elementary school pupils are 65 percent more likely to be bullied by their peers, whereas overweight adolescents are 13 percent more likely to be bullied.

While youngsters are more concerned with their looks than ever before, adolescence is still the worst age for appreciating one's physique. Between the ages of 12 and 15, the average person's body image reaches an all-time low, and so does self-esteem. According to studies, many girls may abandon various activities during the adolescent years, such as traveling to the beach, participating in sports, or even speaking in public, due to concerns about their looks.

With the decline in body image during adolescence comes an increased risk of eating disorders. The majority of eating issues develop in adolescence. Unhealthy eating habits are frequent even among kids who may not have a full-fledged eating problem. Half of the adolescent females and one-third of adolescent boys fast, binge, or utilize smoking, laxatives, or extreme exercise to regulate their weight.

Evidence suggests that media, such as movies, television, publications, and social media, plays a significant role in teen body dissatisfaction. According to studies, the more time young women spend on social media, the more likely they have a negative body image.

Girls are six times more likely to participate in unhealthy eating when they read articles on diets and weight loss, whereas boys are four times more likely. Over 90% of adolescent females believe that the media encourages them to be skinny. While 65% believe fashion models are excessively thin, 46% aspire to appear like the images they see in fashion publications

Body Image and Gender

People of all genders are affected by body image concerns. While many people believe that messages about weight and attractiveness have a greater impact on women than on males, this is changing. In the early 1990s, 15% of teenage guys were dissatisfied with their physique.

This figure has now risen to nearly 45 percent. A recent survey of college-age guys discovered that more than 90% of them disliked at least one feature of their physique.

Boys nowadays are torn between wanting to be slimmer and wanting to be more muscular. As a result, men's body image concerns may manifest differently from women's. Many lads go to the gym to bulk up and slip into routines of unhealthy food and excessive activity. To make matters worse, males are less likely than women to seek therapy for body image concerns, even when their health is at stake.

Men and women suffer from body dysmorphia in similar proportions, but men are significantly less likely to seek therapy.

In persons of either gender, having a negative body image may lead to a loss of self-esteem and self- confidence and an increased risk of depression, anxiety, and eating disorders. If you're unhappy with your physique, you should know that treatment is available. If you're struggling with body image concerns, talk to your doctor or call the National Eating Disorders Hotline at (800) 931-2237

Continue reading for more tips on how to enhance your body image.

How to Overcome a Poor Body Image

If you have a negative body image, working on it will help you improve your physical and mental health and wellness, boost your self-esteem and self-confidence, and make it easier to form meaningful connections with those around you. If you're ready to start working on changing your body image, the tools listed below may be useful.

Recognize that your body image changes.

Begin your journey to a healthy lifestyle by accepting that body image changes and varies naturally day to day, month - to - month.

There might require some practice to settle your negative thoughts about your physical, and then there will never be a point when you have finished the process of developing a positive body image. Doubt and concern might always return.

It's critical to recognize that appreciating your body is a process. Understanding this can help you get back on track if your trip becomes disrupted.

Self-Compassion should be practiced.

Maintaining a good body image in the Face of a society that stresses physical attractiveness at every turn through literature, television, and interactions with friends and family is difficult. Fortunately, research on women shows that fostering self-compassion can aid in maintaining a healthy body image in the Face of negative societal pressures. Self-compassion is simply the practice of being compassionate to oneself.

To improve your self-compassion, read Self-Compassion by Dr. Kristen Neff, the psychologist who pioneered self-compassion research. The book is chock-full of exercises to help you cultivate your sense of self-compassion.

Cognitive-Behavioral Therapy (CBT)

Cognitive-behavioral therapy (CBT) is a form of treatment that focuses on teaching patients effective skills for dealing with negative thoughts and behaviors. CBT

One of the most often utilized therapy for improving body image, CBT teaches you how to identify and modify the thoughts, feelings, and behaviors that contribute to your poor body image.

If you want to attempt CBT, the Association for Behavioral and Cognitive Therapies maintains a registry of trained therapists online.

While meeting with a therapist is the most effective approach to learning to manage negative thought patterns, you may also do measures at home. Try the following if you find yourself obsessing over your body:

- Work through Thomas Cash's Body Image Workbook. This book contains several research-proven techniques that can assist you in dealing with your poor body image.

- Eliminate negative body language. We critique our own and other people's bodies much too often. Decide to put a stop to this negativity. Stop yourself whenever you begin to speak or think something bad about anyone's physique - your own or someone else's – and replace it with something good. Then it might take some time, but if you persist with them, you will learn to leap immediately to the excellent ideas and leave the poor ones behind.

- Make the mirror your ally. Many of us have a strained connection with our reflection. We'll either ignore it totally or exploit it to point out our weaknesses or make fun of ourselves. Instead, decide to be kind and nice to the person in the mirror. Look yourself in the eyes when you see your reflection. Smile. Wave. Say something kind, encouraging, or enticing. Make nice notes for yourself and place them in the mirror frame. Don't allow yourself to grimace at your mirror or criticize your looks in any way.

- Engage in mindfulness meditation. It has been shown that as little as 10 minutes of mindfulness meditation each day might assist in quieting negative thinking patterns and increasing mood. Meditation may also teach you to be more present in your body and listen to its demands.

All you have now is a peaceful place to relax and a few minutes to get started. There are several free or low- cost meditation applications for your smartphone, or you may try following along with a basic meditation video on YouTube. Simply choose someone whose voice you enjoy and follow their directions.

Improve Your Media Literacy

Advertisements for weight-loss drugs, articles were diving into an advanced diet, exercise, beauty regimes, and social media postings featuring gorgeous individuals with flawless skin and hair. All three — the commercials, the

articles, and the social postings – are frequently meticulously tailored to sell you something.

In the case of social media, what is frequently marketed is the illusion that the person in the photo is lovely and carefree, regardless of reality? It might be difficult to feel good about your physique when comparing your everyday self in the mirror to the flawless snapshot an influencer just uploaded. Learning about the different ways in which pictures may be altered, filtered, and manipulated, on the other hand, can help you comprehend the difference between truth and reality in images, as well as make you feel better about yourself.

To understand more about media literacy and its relationship to body image, go to About Face, which provides online media literacy training for teenagers (but useful for adults). The Canadian non-profit Media Smarts also provides extensive media literacy tools, including courses on food advertising, media and body image, gender stereotypes in the media, and more. Furthermore, the National Eating Disorders Association provides a media literacy toolbox.

Curate Your Media With Care

Even if you are aware of how media images attempt to affect you, it is still necessary to be informed about the information you consume. Support films, TV shows, periodicals, and websites feature people of all ages, genders, body kinds, and abilities. Unfollow influencers that make you feel horrible about yourself on social media and seek out voices who discuss relevant subjects.

Accept Healthy Movement

Workouts are among the most important thing you can do for your health, fitness, and mental wellbeing. If you are not a daily exerciser, choose the activity you enjoy and start doing it.

If you inspire yourself to exercise by creating objectives, make sure they are positive and related to your abilities, fitness, and enjoyment, rather than goals centered on reducing weight or inches. Mastering a new skill, jogging a new distance, or boosting your lifting capacity are all examples of good objectives. Setting healthy, positive objectives for your body and witnessing it grow stronger and more skillful may improve your relationship with your body image.

Mind-body sports like yoga and tai chi may teach you to connect with and appreciate your body. Olympic weightlifting, dancing, ice skating, rock climbing, or a new-to-you team activity can also improve your body image.

You'll get new respect for your body and what it can achieve if you focus on acquiring new abilities and see your slow but steady growth as you continue to practice your chosen activity.

Discover More About Nutrition

Any newsstand (or website) will have hundreds of headlines on every diet under the sun, interspersed with recipes for cookies, cakes, pies, and BBQs. It's overwhelming and perplexing. Did you realize that the Keto, Atkins, Paleo, and low-carb diets are essentially the same thing? If the media is your sole source of information, it might be difficult for the normal individual to decide what to consume. You won't be as healthy as you may be if your diet isn't ideal, and your body image may suffer as a result.

Avoid fashion and fitness publications if you want trustworthy, science-based dietary information. The diet information included inside may be inaccurate or even hazardous. Research suggests that even casually reading a fashion magazine reduces your body image. Visit My Plate, the USDA's nutrition website, instead. It gives straightforward dietary suggestions.

Consider consulting with a licensed nutritionist (RD) if you still require assistance. RDs will teach you the fundamentals of good eating and nourish your body with nutritious, enjoyable foods that will keep you healthy and bright.

Live for the Present, Not the Future

It's all too easy to succumb to body image concerns in today's media-saturated atmosphere. More than half of all people dislike some part of their bodies. This has major ramifications. A poor body image raises your chances of developing mental health problems and prevents you from attaining your objectives and goals.

Many people who are unhappy with their physique put off doing activities they want to accomplish until they obtain the "ideal figure."

The problem is that the ideal body does not exist. Happiness, on the other hand, does. If you've been putting off going on vacation, going to the beach, or doing anything else until you attain a specific body ideal, it's time to quit waiting to be perfect and start living now. After all, being happy with your body is the greatest way to be pleased with your body.

MAKE IT HAPPEN

MAKE IT HAPPEN

HOW TO STOP MAKING EXCUSES AND ACHIEVE YOUR GOAL

Introduction: The Goals That Never Happen

How many unfinished goals do you presently have on your to-do list? Suppose you're like the great majority of us. In that case, you probably have hundreds of projects that you began but never finished, innumerable objectives that you promised your friends but never followed through on, and a variety of ambitions that seem less and less likely to come true.

As a result, when you tell folks about your "next big endeavor," they may roll their eyes. When you begin a new weight-loss exercise program and everyone – including you – knows you're likely to lose interest by month two.

Or while discussing the app, you want to create, the website, or the company idea. Or when you mention your long-awaited vacation to Japan...

For many of us, this is the norm. We work tremendously hard at things we don't care about, only to put food on the table, yet we are shockingly ineffective when it comes to realizing our ambitions.

It's time to alter all of that and start making those dreams a reality. But how do you turn things around?

How We'll Fix Your Goal Setting and Assist You in Living the Life of Your Dreams

Having accomplished objectives is about strategy, making a psychiatric and psychological, changing the way you think, and being strategic about approaching each goal. It's also important to understand how to pick your goals and even frame them.

You'll learn how to identify and develop successful objectives, how to create effective action plans, and how to stay on track and never give up.

But, like other goal-setting books, this one will be a bit different. After giving you the basic tools you need to start creating and achieving your objectives, we'll look at how you can start putting them into action.

Because, while a goal may be very about anything, it will fall into one of many categories for many of us. Most of us have objectives for our relationships, for our fitness, for our employees, and our travel. We'll provide you not just the abstract methods you'll need to start setting effective objectives but also the step- by-step processes you'll need to put these strategies into action in each of these areas. By the conclusion of this book, you'll be able to establish and achieve any objective. At the same time, you'll have effective tactics for enhancing your relationships, fitness, job, and other areas.

Are you ready to make a positive change in your life?

CHAPTER 1: THE FORMULA – HOW TO STRUCTURE GOALS AND MAKE YOUR PLAN

Now that you understand the fundamentals of what constitutes a good goal, it's time to start setting these sorts of objectives for yourself. This chapter will set out some easy steps you may take to start putting these concepts into action.

Later, we'll apply this same approach to various aspects of your life, so you may start pursuing a better body, a better salary, and a better love life. But in each case, we'll employ the same method.

Step 1: Visualize

The first and most critical stage is imagining and fully comprehending what you desire. We've previously touched on this briefly in terms of being wealthy. Often, it is not the money itself that you desire, but rather what that money signifies in terms of your lifestyle or position.

The same is true for physical fitness. It's not enough to desire to be slimmer or healthier; you also need to understand why you want to be that way. Do you aspire to be a more physically proficient person, perhaps even a professional athlete? Do you wish to avoid the degeneration that many people suffer as they become older? Or do you want to appear great to be more successful with the other sex?

Visualizing your future is typically the greatest approach to acquiring a sense of what you want out of life in any particular area. That entails shutting your eyes and imagining your perfect future. Where have you gone? How do you appear? What precisely is it that you do for a living? What exactly are you doing?

By seeing your future in this abstract form, you'll be able to begin analyzing what you're truly attempting to achieve, and from there, you'll be able to begin looking at the more specific measures you'd need to take to get there.

Other approaches that may be used to aid with this are as follows:

- Examining your role models to determine what they have in common

- Consider the things that motivate you, your interests, the things you enjoy, and so on.

- Consider the last time you felt genuinely joyful or alive. From and where it is, it's also a good time to consider the actual reality and imagine what it's like to go there and live that life. Do you still desire it?

For illustrate, it's quite simple to desire to be a professional musician in theory. Still, you might not enjoy the actual lifestyle: traveling, being in the public glare, and presumably trying to raise a family.

This is why we're thinking in terms of abstractions right now. Because you could discover that the reality of being a rock star isn't something you desire - in which case you'll have to start over and figure out what this was about that lifestyle that drew you in. Is it possible to achieve the same emotional goals in different ways? If you want to be known for your music, consider strumming chords on Videos or Band Camp! A classically trained musician could write music for computer games or videos if that is all that you want to do.

But it doesn't have to be all concerning your job. You might also find that you enjoy busking or making music in your free time.

If you can get to the heart of what you don't like, it might also help you get over seemingly impossible obstacles. Even if you want to be an astronaut one day, you might have to accept the fact that you are already too old and that it's now very unlikely that you will ever be able to. However, consider why that appeals to you on an emotional level. Maybe it boils down to your love of space, in which case you'd be just as happy as an astronomer? Perhaps it boils down to your passion for adventure and discovery, in which case you could be an explorer or just a researcher.

Step 2: Evaluate Your Situation Sincerity and thoroughness

The following critical step is to compare your existing situation to the ideal one you have imagined. This is where you'll analyze the gap between real life and your ideal future and try to figure out the best approach to bridge it.

Making an honest assessment of your existing circumstances is a critical step in determining your current position and, as a result, your strengths and limitations.

And, in particular, you should consider what advantages you have, what networks you have, what contacts you have, and what opportunities you have. You may believe you have none, but this is most likely due to a lack of thoroughness. Adage: There is no shortage of resources, only a lack of resourcefulness, which is what it means to say that.

This is also where you'll assess the likelihood of your goals and, if necessary, re-evaluate them. If you've determined that you're not likely to become an astronaut, it's time to choose a more realistic aim, such as becoming an astronomer.

If your goal is to date very gorgeous women, it's time to rethink your strategy and, at the very least, begin by aiming for ladies on a similar level to yourself.

This step's philosophy should be to honestly examine your circumstances and follow the "way of least resistance." You want to get a lot done in the least amount of time and effort.

Step 3: Create a Strategy

This leads us to the following phase: creating a strategy based on your current status, where you want to go, and the possibilities accessible to you.

Looking at different training regimens, for example, can help you lose weight or become in shape. However, by doing an honest evaluation of yourself and your circumstances in the last phase, you should be better positioned to select a system that appeals to your specific strengths and limitations and that you are likely to follow through on.

So many individuals are willing to pay for pricey training programs that include following a strict diet and working out ten times each week for an hour. Is it, however, a reasonable expectation? If you've attempted and failed to stick to past workouts, the answer is most likely no.

When you evaluate your present circumstances, you must also consider them. It's important to think about how things have gone wrong in the past, as well as what your current lifestyle and personality can handle.

And once you know this, you may hunt for or create a training program that will benefit you. Perhaps it means finding a method to include a CV into your daily routine, or perhaps it involves keeping to a diet that you will find pleasurable and easy.

The same is true for vacation and career ambitions. It's time to come down to earth and get your head out of the clouds. Instead of fantasizing about traveling the world, consider how you will travel more despite your commitments, financial constraints, and so on. Stop wishing you were wealthy and start thinking about how you're going to climb the corporate ladder to get there.

When creating your strategy, it's also crucial to go outside the box and reject commonly held views about what you need to do to achieve each objective.

Reject the Status Quo

Because we are only taught one method to acquire what we desire, that is to advance in our jobs. This is why so many of us become trapped. We decide to be wealthy, so we work more, rather than recognizing that we might be wealthy on our existing incomes by spending less and maybe earning a secondary income. We believe that the only way to succeed in music is to continue doing our day jobs to pay for it. We believe that the only way to travel more is to work more and retire sooner.

However, your living expenses will surely rise to meet your wage, you will have less and less time as you work more and take on more responsibility, and you will discover that there is never a 'good moment' to achieve your goals.

As a result, you must take the road less traveled. The way you get where you want to go isn't the only way. If you're just hitting your head against a brick wall, it's time to change your plan.

Nothing prevents you from launching a company in your leisure time right now. There's no reason you can't quit your work and travel right away. You have the skills required to begin applying for higher-paying employment. What's holding you back?

Step 4: Break Your Goals Down Into Smaller Steps

You're going to hone in now that you know what you want to achieve and how you want to get there. As you now understand the "big picture," it's time to pay attention to the small details.

You know you want to be in shape; you know going to the gym isn't an option for you, and doing out from home makes a lot more sense.

So all that remains is to frame this as a goal that you can work toward every day or week. As a result, "I shall exercise for at least 15 minutes every day."

Maybe you've decided you don't want to tone your muscles and instead want to lose weight so you can look better in a suit and feel more active. In such a scenario, your objective maybe something like, "I will walk to and from work every day that it isn't raining."

And there is nothing or have more than one objective or setting more specific goals. You may pair this with a secondary aim, such as "I will not consume anything on my 'items to avoid list.'"

Concentrate on these modest actions to get closer to your objective one step at a time. Similarly, if you want to develop in your job, you may set a goal of "using any chance that occurs to better my CV."

Or

"Apply for one evening job three times a week."

Some of your larger ambitions will need many steps. For example, if you want to become a famous musician, you should consider the following steps:

Learn to play the guitar in half an hour each evening, four days a week. Save $15 per day to invest in studio equipment. Produce one video per week to create an audience. Produce two videos per week to grow an audience.

Continue to release two videos every week and spend one hour per week on self-promotional efforts. Spend two hours per week working on an album to sell through the channel.

It's a time-consuming procedure, but it's also a viable one. It is a plan that you must employ if you want to succeed. It reflects a cognitive change in which you no longer daydream about being a renowned rock star and instead focus on tangible, realistic, and attainable tasks.

That's when you'll start making genuine, tangible progress!

CHAPTER 2: LETTING GO OF FEAR

Inside, you may already know this.

It makes sense that you should take small, concrete steps to reach your goals instead of making big plans like "become a rock star" or "get richer."

So, why haven't you been able to do that? There are two things:

1) It takes a lot of work. It's easier and far more pleasant to dream big and get the benefit that comes with that than to face the reality of working hard to achieve your goals. We'll communicate about this more as the book goes on when we talk about how to stay positive and keep traveling, however, when things get hard.

When you feel like it's not the right time to do something, you don't do it. Instead, you put things off and look for other jobs. Again, this only needs a little rocket fuel, which we'll look at later.

Then, you're scared. When I see this, I think it's why so many of us have boring and boring lives. Risk-taking and putting yourself out there. We don't want to do that. It's easier to describe ourselves as very productive and pretend we'll do another one than it does to put ourselves out there and consider getting our egos broken when things don't go our way.

We're about to talk about the second thing. If you want to succeed, you can't keep putting things off! The best way to tell if you're procrastinating is to look at your work.

Some examples of procrastination are:

• The woman spent so much time reading books and investigating the subject instead of just getting started, which most people do. As someone who wants to get fit, I see this a lot all the time. So many people spend a lot of time reading books and blogs about fitness programs, hiring consultants, and buying gym clothes to help them get in shape. That's the only thing they don't do. It's time to start working out. That doesn't mean that you shouldn't look into health and fitness, of course! Even though it should be praised, it should be. The difficulty is when you use this as an excuse to not work out. The truth is that any kind of training is better than none at all. Start doing strength exercises and pull-ups right now if you want to start getting in shape. There is no reason not to. You can strengthen your routine over time if you start now, but you need to start now.

• When you work on projects and don't finish them, I'm an app developer, and I've made about $90,000 from two very popular apps that I've made in the past. Not enough to change your life over a few years, but enough to make your life a little more comfortable, especially as they keep making money while you work your regular job. Enough that, many people say that they want to make a good app, too. Work on it for three years, but they don't let anyone see it. Because I'm different from them. As soon as my app was a "minimum viable product," I put it on the market. Later, we'll talk more about the "fail fast approach," which we're going to do now.

On the other hand, I put myself out there while they made excuses. Perfectionism is often just a way to put things off. Check yourself out!

Claim the time is not right. The time is never right. What is the reason you aren't going to the beach right now? Save up some money, but by then, you'll likely be in a good place with your job and not want to take a break. Then you'll have a friend and not want to leave them behind. A child will follow. For example, there is never the right time to start a relationship or get married. You should also never start a business or start a new job at the right time. You always do it, no matter what. Then what should we do? Asked forgiveness, not permission, is how you should go about it at that time. What might happen after you finish? There is nothing else you can do.

I was not paying attention to how unhappy you were. No, I don't think I do. I know someone who clearly wants to be in a relationship but instead focuses on their job. Every

How happy they are about their new job, or how much they enjoy their trips. But don't you think they just want to go home to someone? Many people try to cover up a gap in their lives by focusing on another. Because they have a family, some people don't want to go after their dream job. That's great. But why not do

Step 1: Visualize

The first and most critical stage is imagining and fully comprehending what you desire. We've previously touched on this briefl both? Because your story will inspire your students, this is the best way. You need to be super pleased in every aspect of everyday life to be truly happy. Do not make this mistake! Don't do this.

Fear setting in

If you still can't get past these psychological barriers, Tim Ferriss has a "fear setting" technique that you can use in his book, "The Four Hour Workweek." This technique is called "fear setting."

To start, you're going to write down all of the things that are holding you back and things you're afraid of. Then, you're going to write down counterarguments, contingency plans, and more to remove those fears.

Take some moment to think about your goals and dreams, then write down all the things you want to do. Write down your goals and steps to get there. Take a moment to think about taking that first step now. Is there anything stopping you from going? What are you afraid of? The best way to be truthful and thorough is to include all of the possible problems that could happen.

Suppose that you want to start your own business. This is what you're worried about and afraid of:

To buy a business, you do not have enough money. You might lose your job and not be able to find work in the future, leading to your family struggling and you losing your home. Your business might fail and make you look like a failure, making your partner think you are unreasonable and posing complications in your relationship.

Now, look at each of these oppositions and think about how likely they are or how you can deal with them or avoid them.

As an example:

It's not that you don't have money.

Taking out a loan may be risky and put you in a lot of debt if the business doesn't work out.

Consider a PayPal loan, which is a loan that you pay back only with PayPal income. This means that you won't owe anything until you start making money. You can also try Kickstarter.

You would perhaps lose your job and not have a steady source of income if you don't even have a rainy day fund. You might not be able to find work in the future, which could lead to your family dying of starvation and you ruining your life. In most cases, your employer will give you your job back if you need it. At the very least, you could perhaps likely discover lower-level effort to keep you going - even if that means just doing a portion job.

It doesn't matter what other people think. The bad thing you can do is not try to make anything of yourself or follow your dreams.

Okay, so now we can begin creating progress in the aspects of living that you want to prevent.

CHAPTER 3: HOW YOU CAN MAKE YOUR FITNESS GOALS COME TO PAST

Here are the basics of how to reach your general goals. Now it's time to reach specific goals. For this chapter, we're going to talk about fitness and how you can use the principles we've talked about to get in great shape, so stay tuned!

It's important to figure out why you want to get fit and what you want that to look and feel like. You want to get fit so you can play sports again. Do you want to look good for your pleasure? If so, do you want to be strong so that you look more intimidating to other people? Do you want to be more healthy? Or could they be attracted to people of the opposite sex?

And how are you currently? What have you tried before? Why hasn't it worked? It's important to know how you look now. Physically, what are your strengths, and what are your best traits? What are you good at? When do you have it?

This is very important because it will change how you go about getting your goals done.

In this case, you might decide that bulking up is the best way to become more physically intimidating. To become a tank, you need to add as much mass as quickly as possible. It means eating a lot of calories and a lot of protein, taking many breaks, and lifting heavy weights.

People who are trying to get more women's attention by becoming more toned and lean will want to eat less and do more aerobic exercise like walking or running to do this.

Another thing you should consider is which exercises you like to do and which exercises can be done in a way that is easy for you to do. You also need to think about any physical limitations, like illnesses or joint problems.

This ebook will tell you how to set and achieve realistic goals.

One of the most important things to think about when developing a training plan is whether or not it goes into your daily life. Observe how you feel at different times of the day and think about how you can use free time in your schedule to train, for example.

Putting it together In

Watch how you feel at separate moments of the week and presume about how you can use your unlimited time to train, for example.

Putting things together In

You can lose weight by taking more walks. To lose weight, you should walk. Many calories are burned without making you tired or sweaty, and it doesn't make you sweaty. You don't have to make it too hard as you can fit it in with your other plans.

It's also very easy for most of us to add more walking to our daily schedules. For example, you might be able to go for a long walk during your lunch break at work. There are 60 minutes at lunch. You can eat for 10 minutes and walk for the rest. It's best to walk at the end. A 50-minute walk each day should be enough to meet your 10,000-step goal, which is about 5 miles and should burn an extra 3,000 calories each week. If you normally burn many calories, that's how many you should burn in a day. The most important thing is improving your health, giving you more sunlight and fresh air, and more.

Try not to do HIIT workouts five times a week that leave you sore. Instead, go for a nice walk that will easily fit into your schedule.

If you get off the bus early or walk home from work, you can also get a walk-in.

The same is true for diet, as well. I always tell my clients to follow a strict diet only in the morning and lunch. Why? Because most of us want to have fun meals with our partners at the end of the day. Or we want to go out with our friends and eat pudding while we're out with them.

However, when it comes to main meals, they tend to be more useful than fancy. Often, they are eaten alone and quickly. You can cut back on carbohydrates or carbs at this time of day. And after that, in the evening, you can do the same thing.

Then, think about how you would make this convenient for yourself and other people. Protein shakes are sold in bottles at a shop every morning, so you might want to give up your morning coffee for a protein shake. This is great if you don't want to mix your protein shake and spill it all over the floor because you don't want to eat it.

Then, if you can't get to the gym, you could work out at home. You could also start swimming if your office has a pool nearby.

Laugh about it.

Your exercise should be something you enjoy, not something you hate. You can't build lean muscle with weights if you've tried and failed to do so. This isn't what you're into, so it doesn't make sense.

That's not the only thing we should do. We should all find some kind of exercise we enjoy. So, do you think you should get a pair of parallel bars? They're cheap, and you can do gymnastics or hand-balancing at home.

If you want to do something, you could try rock climbing. People who like to climb rocks are great at building big, strong muscles, especially in their lats and forearms. Is there a chance you'll fall in love with boxing? If so, getting a heavy bag is a great way to build big shoulders in a fun way. Or, you might not be a good powerlifter.

Find a way to learn, no matter what. All of the most powerful people and people with the best bodies have in common. Their favorite thing is getting bigger. Their favorite things are getting chalk on their hands and hanging out with other swole people. They eat, sleep, and plan about the gym.

Find out what makes you excited about the end goal and the journey to get there.

You should play to your strengths.

A lot of people are naturally ectomorphs, but not everyone is. This determines whether you're a big, bulky person or a lean person who "hard gains" a lot of weight.

There are times when your goals should be in line with your natural strengths (remember step 2?). When you are an endomorph, you can work on becoming a huge, powerful hulk. Why not try out the lean look that a lot of people like?

As long as you can be flexible, you should go for the one you're already good at. If you do this, the results will come more quickly, which means that you'll start to enjoy the process more.

Another option you can do is look for people who are like you. Seek out people who started in the same situation as you. People with the same body types can make the most of what they have. To get training advice from them is a good idea because they have probably worked with the same genetic starting point and had the same set of circumstances in their lives to start with.

Take it easy.

A good goal for fitness should be to work out for at least 15 minutes, or maybe even 10 minutes. You don't want to come up with crazy ideas like training twice a day because you'll gain muscle quickly and lose it quickly. To avoid getting tired, be willing to see small changes over time.

However, don't take it so long that you won't see any progress. MED stands for "Minimum Effective Dose." The goal here is to use the MED. To put it another way, you're giving yourself just enough time to see progress so that you can start to think about your strategy and improve it over time. Take care not to do more or less.

* * *

Then you should have emerged with a coaching formula that includes you, your lifestyle, and your genes after you did all this.

Try to start weightlifting again. Anyone may have tried and failed before. Then you might want to try this again. After work, you could go boating three times a week. Or you could get a heavy bag and punch it for 40 minutes a few times a week. Do 15 minutes of press-ups before you go to bed, and then you'll be ready for bed.

Do something right away, no matter what, and then try different things until you find what works best for you.

CHAPTER 4: HOW YOU CAN MAKE YOUR CAREER GOALS HAPPEN

Too many people have bad ideas about how to go about their jobs. Adults often think that working very hard in jobs that we don't enjoy is good. This is not always true, though. We often think that we don't choose what we do for a living. We are often afraid to try new things.

It might be because people just "let things happen" and take the position that comes their way. This makes them unhappy with their jobs. The first job that comes our way when researchers finish education is what we should take. This is what we should do. Then, we work hard to move up the ladder. Ask yourself: Is this what I want? We don't do that. Is there anything I can do?

Here are some ways to use the principles we've talked about to make progress in your job.

When you know what you want, you can get it.

You should start with step 3 – coming up with your plan. It's time to accept that you don't have to keep working at a job you don't like, and there's no reason to even care about your job at all.

There is a myth that you need to get your sense of satisfaction and progress from your job. We need to get rid of that first, so That means that you should get the same amount of pleasure from a hobby. How we think about ourselves is often linked to how well we do at work. We often think this means we have to work even harder and work even longer to feel like we're making progress in our jobs.

Life. As CEO of a logistics company, you still have to make sure people get staplers, even though you might be more interested in painting.

This is why it's often better to shift your attention to your "extra-curricular activities." My sister did this as an artist when she realized that her dream job (making movie props) wasn't as romantic as she thought it would be. When that didn't work out, she took a job to pay the bills by working as a saleswoman. Then she used her free time to make her things in her own time.

Since then, she has gained a lot of followers on social media and sold a few pieces for cash. So even though her job isn't something she's very excited about, she still feels like she's making progress and is excited about the future. She doesn't need to take on more responsibilities to be happy and fulfilled.

And that also brings us to another point: your wealth isn't entirely based on your job, either. Whether you rent out your room or cut the hair of your neighbors, you can still make extra funds to help pay for your bills.

This is why it's so important to think about the exact nature of your goals. If your goal is to be richer, you can do it by cutting back on expenses, finding new income skills, and so on. In this case, if you want to rise in the ranks, then you might be happy to keep moving up in your job. If you want to be successful as an artist or get credit for your ideas, you may work on projects outside of the office.

As you can see, this is what we call "lifestyle design." People interested in lifestyle design are looking for ways to get where they want to go and how to get there with the least amount of work. Is taking on a "menial" job a good idea? It might not be the best way to get more done in other parts of your life.

How about making money from somewhere else so that you can work only four days a week? That could be the case. What the heck!

Creating a fool-proof plan

Fright can have a lot of power over us. We've talked about how it can stop us from pursuing our dreams. This is especially true for getting things done in our jobs. Because of that, it makes sense for us to look at some of the things we can do to make our job goals less risky.

Many people say they want to look for a new job but can't because they have too many obligations. They might even say that if they didn't look, they wouldn't be able to find another job that paid the same.

As long as you don't see this as a risky thing and don't get scared when you look for work, the simple answer is to just look for other jobs while you're still at work. There is no risk at all if you spend a few evenings looking at other jobs and applying for them. You can only leave your current job when you have a new one.

The same is true if you start a part-time business. To start a new business, you don't have to move from one job to another right away. You can work on your new business idea in your spare time at night or the weekends. When you are sure it works, should you think about leaving your current job and taking on the new one? This will give you another risk-free way to move to a job or career you love.

You could even cut back on your work hours and use the extra time to work on your business. In your free time, do work on your business project.

When it comes to investing, the same thing is true. To get money for your business idea, there are many risk- free ways. Kickstarter, for example, is a great way to start a business these days because there is no risk, and it's a good way to see how people will react to your idea.

You could also ask your parents for money, get a business partner from a friend, or get a credit card loan to start your own business. There's no need to quit your job to get a new one. You can just make sure that the loan repayment terms are something you could pay off even if your job was lost. That way, you won't be putting yourself in any danger.

To make this happen, you have to want it.

If you know what you want to be when you grow up and you just want to be a rock musician, don't get distracted by the idea of making money. Make sure you start by focusing on what you love and making more time for it. Let success happen as a byproduct of what you do.

It is rewarding when you start working on your project right away. You'll also find that it wakes you up in the morning because you now have a drive and passion for it that makes you excited to be around other people. It doesn't even matter if you're a winner. If you fail, don't be afraid to change your strategy and try something else. It's impossible to fail when you do this.

Taking the path with the least amount of work

It's important to remember that going for what you want means taking the most direct and practical route to get there. This is titled the path with the least amount of work. In this case, that means coming up with a business idea that you can do or making one that fits your contacts and ideas.

It's one thing that many people do wrong. They come up with ideas they think will change the world. There's no need to start making money if that is your goal.

But if your goal was to become rich, or maybe become financially independent, then the best way to achieve that goal is to focus on proven ways to make money.

That means that you don't have to break the mold and develop new business models. There isn't any need to be the next Mark Zuckerberg in exchange for doing well at your job. So many big projects fail each year because there are billions of them each year.

At the same time, look at how many successful businesses there are in the world of shopping, clotheslines, resale, building, and hairstyling. Following through with a good idea that you've seen work isn't bad. You now have a plan for success, and you don't have to start from scratch.

Think about your resources and contacts, too. Make the most of it if you know the editor of a gardening magazine. You can start a gardening service and advertise with them. This is a very good thing to do.

Make sure to use your strengths, and if gardening is one of them, this is a good job for you. Starting your own business is often a good idea if you stay in your current field. This way, you will have the knowledge, experience, and contacts you need to get a good head start on your new business.

Remember step 2: figuring out where you are now and what you have. Everything you have, your skills, and your limitations should be on the list. What variations can you make in your business and technology to help you get more done?

The Fail Fast Model is a way to ensure that you fail quickly.

Remember when we talked about how some people are afraid of failing? One way this happened was when someone worked on their product for a long time without putting it out there. If your product doesn't work out when you release it, you could lose everything if it doesn't work out the way you planned. This happened to a person who did this.

A friend of mine came up with an idea for a business and worked on it for three years to make it better. He trademarked the business name, hired a lawyer, and even paid for a fancy launch party! All for what was just a website. Every browser and every screen size was tested to the letter. He did a lot of market research and paid for a lot of server space and bandwidth to handle the coming traffic. But his upfront and long-term costs were so high that he went broke almost right away.

The "fail fast model" is the opposite of this. If you have an idea for a business, you should make an MVP or "minimal viable product." This is what you should do first. This one is a simple, cheap, and easy version of your product or service that you can start selling right away. Because of this, you can now try it out without spending a lot of time and money on it. Many ideas are put on the wall, and quickly something works. If the idea works out, you can spend more time and money on it. If it isn't, you try again, learn from your mistakes, and move on to the next thing!

CHAPTER 5: HOW YOU CAN MAKE YOUR RELATIONSHIP GOALS HAPPEN

To what kind of trip do you want to go? What if you want to see the world? Again, we follow our steps, which means we think about the kind of travel we want to do and then figure out a way to make it happen that works for us and our situation.

Imagine the type of travel you want to do, think about the things you want to get from your trip, and how you can reach those bigger goals. This is how we start again.

Next, look at your situation and see what you can do. What is stopping you? Is there a budget limit? Responsibility for the family? Fear? In this case, make your plans and break them down into small steps. Even if you think outside the box and take a different path to success, you might still be on the right track. Taking a gap year and traveling to different parts of the world isn't always the best way to get a job.

Alternative ways to travel

It may be that you will not have the time and money for that because you'll get just as much out of going on a trip closer to home instead. There are many great things to see and do in the US. The whole of the EU is on your doorstep if you live in America. This can be just as exciting and different, even if it's not what you thought it would be. The way you thought it would work out isn't going to be what it is. But it will still make you want to go out and look for new things.

Or, how about just going for a shorter amount of time instead? Life-changing events can happen in just three or two months. And you're more likely to get time off from work that long and be prepared to save them money, too. You can indeed try taking a series of private trips all year long instead of one big trip at a time. This might also be possible to convince a partner off than going on a long trip for months at a time, like going on a cruise.

When it comes to money, you might be surprised at how little you need to travel if you go during the non- peak season, stay on people's couches, or use Air BnB to stay somewhere. That means that you can make a little money online to help pay for your trip, too.

Or, could you ask your current job if you could be sent to another country? If the organization has a presence worldwide, this could be a good idea for them. In the same way, there might be a job that requires you to travel. You could also apply for a job that requires you to travel. People go on retreat to make money and give their other half a reason to be happy.

There is also no explanation you can't take your best friend with you, either.

Conclusions

It's possible to set many different kinds of goals and use this formula to achieve them. Among other things, you might want to keep improving your finances, your home, your social life, or even how you look. Learning a new skill or dressing better could also be on your list.

The whole aspect of this device is that you can use it anywhere, and when you do, it will help you figure out how to get what you want. Dreams become steps you can follow to make them occur. Sometimes, you might have to change your goals to make them a little more attainable, but if you're smart about it, they won't be less rewarding. The very next Brad Pitt or Angelina Jolie might not be in your future. But there's no justification you can't start playing small parts in movies if you think about how to make your life work around auditions.

People who know what they want and then figure out the fastest way to get there are the best. You start to try, and as soon as you do, life gets a lot better and more fun. I think it's time to stop fantasizing and start doing things.

It's time to do it!

MAKE IT HAPPEN
Cheat Sheet

A cheat sheet for attempting to make anything happen. Sounds great, doesn't it? So, to be fair, the cheat sheet will indeed give you the recommendations and the best ways to do things. Make it Happen is a book with many ideas about how to make things happen. These are just some of the ideas from the book. You're going to put them into practice.

– You are the best!

The Formula is

The formula is the most important thing we should take away from the book. These are the four steps you can take to start making positive changes in any part of your life. These four steps:

1. Think about your passion.

2. Take a look at your current situation.

3. Think of a way to win.

4. Decide on small steps. Then, let's break this down:

1. This is how you're going to figure out what you want. Imagine what your ideal future looks like and how happy you are. There you are. What are you up to? You're with who? It doesn't matter how hard or weird your goals might be. You need to choose the things that make you the most excited about. Here are some things we didn't talk about in the book, but they can still help you learn about your favorite subject:

2. When were you truly happy? a. Remember when you were joyful. There are a lot of things you like to do. What did you ever think life was like when you were a child?

They all have the same thing.

That would be the second-best thing. Think about where you are now and how straightforward it will be to reach your goals. Do you live near them? Is it because you have tried so far that you haven't been able to move forward? You've done something wrong.

Besides, you should think about your current resources, contracts, and chances. If you don't take the time to think about what you have and how to use it, you won't be able to use it.

Think about it, and then you may not have known what those are.

3. Then, you'll come up with your plan. This will help you get from step 1 to step 2. It will close the gap between what you have and what you want. And it is going to do so logically and systematically, as well. This needs to make sense, be practical, and use everything we learned in step 2. This is a concrete way to get rid of the limitations that have been holding you back and use all of your existing resources simultaneously.

Remember that this might mean going in a different direction to win. Many ways can be used to get what you want in life. You don't have to follow in the footsteps of other people. If you want to be famous, maybe YouTube is a better place to start. But if you want to be rich, you might just be better off following someone else's tried and true method instead.

4. Finally, you'll take that strategy and break it down into small, measurable steps that you can work on a lot. This means that the whetstone is being made. "Train at least 15 minutes, three times a week and." If you should get in shape, that might be your small goal. As a goal, you may want to write one page a night. You might want to post one video a week as a short-term goal.

Make sure you stay on track with these tools:

Most of the time, even if you have the right plan, it can be hard to keep going toward your goals. To keep going or start something new, you will need to use a few more tools and strategies that help because this is why.

Here are some useful tips:

Fear setting in

Fear setting is a way to deal with the fears that might be stopping you from doing something. It starts by writing down your fears on a piece of paper or computer and putting them into words exactly how you think they should be.

This is important because it lets you question your fears and see if they are true. Add next to each one how likely each one is, what you could do to stop it, and what you would do if it did happen.

Reconnecting

Sometimes, it's easy to forget why you're taking small steps. You want to be in great shape, but you don't think about that when you're running at 5 am. This is why it's important to reconnect emotionally with the thing that makes you want to do what you do. Imagination is a good way to picture what you want and feel the emotional hook that will make you want to go after it.

This is how we make our lives better.

The term "lifestyle design" means making changes to your lifestyle so that it better fits your interests, rather than letting things like your job or where you live dictate how you live.

In this case, lifestyle design means getting rid of all the things that make your goals more difficult and adding things that make your goals more easily. As simple as acquiring a washing machine, so you don't have to clean up after eating food.

In the same way, you'll do things over and over again.

You can learn how to keep going, just like you can learn how to do anything else. This is why many writers say that you should make your bed every single morning. When you do this, you will learn how to be more disciplined. When you can do this every day, you should be more likely to work out in the morning or work on your business in the evening.

POWER OF SELF-REFLECTION

How to reflect on your past and make meaning fulling changes

INTRODUCTION

Most of us don't spend some time thinking about what we're doing in life, and that's a mistake. This is usually because we're focusing on big goals, and we're just going through life at a quick pace. Many people realize that they need to know more about themselves than anyone else, but they have hardship finding the time to sit down and think about it. They always say that they don't have time for that.

A way to think about self-reflection is to think of it as a tool that lets you look at your achievements, skills, flaws, and fears. You can also think about it to look at where you are in life and what drives your thoughts. Mental gymnastics with a very good tool for looking at things in more detail is more like. To find out who you are, think about yourself. It can help you start a big change in your life, take important steps for your development, and help you plan. It can also help you calm down, be more confident, figure out your goal, and be more motivated by what you want to do.

Self-reflection causes you to ask yourself a set of questions. These questions help you figure out what you need to do and lead to more important questions, even though they're very simple. People who ask these questions can do a lot of good for them, too. They can help you work on your small bad habits and help you focus on good things, too.

- Thoughts will help you improve in your weaker areas as they become more clear to your mind. Are there things that I can't change?
- There's a good chance that I don't pay any attention to my goals or tasks.

- There is a chance that I have been negatively thinking about things.

- Do I know that what I do to my body affects my mind? Am I taking care of my body the right way if I know this?

- Are some opinions or facts that I don't think about enough to decide if I agree with or don't agree with

- Do I need to work on any skills?

- In what areas do I need to improve?

- Some of my thoughts aren't true. What do these people think?

- Is this something I know?

- To reach my goals, have I been putting anything back?

- Do I know what I need to do to improve?

It's possible that we could go on and on and on with the list of questions that you can ask yourself. There are so many. This book helps you understand how important self-reflection is. It also gives you a good idea of the tangible benefits of self-reflection and its intricacies. There are ways to reflect properly and let go of the past to be more focused on the present.

CHAPTER 1: UNDERSTANDING SELF-REFLECTION AND ITS SIGNIFICANCE

Every day, we have a lot of chances to show ourselves how much we care about ourselves. Whether we're window shopping or looking in the mirror, we have a lot of chances to admire ourselves and see how beautiful and amazing we are. But we should also think about how wonderful it would be if we could spend a little time shining a little light on our consciousness and look beyond our skin-deep appearances and outer legging-clad texts. Self-reflection is very important when we're looking at our goals and actions. The question is, how often do we think about self-reflection? What about our feelings and gut feelings? How often do we check up on them?

It's a way to think about yourself.

When you take the time to think about your emotions, performance, behaviors, and thoughts to improve and grow, you're self-reflecting. Most of us don't spend some time thinking about what we're doing in life, and that's a mistake. We don't know that when we take the time to think about ourselves, we can make sure that our dreams for the future, gut feelings, and current goals are in line with our path.

With self-reflection, you'll be able to understand the complicated relationship between your goals and emotions, as well as how it can help you be more satisfied with your relationships, be more productive at your daily tasks, be better orientated, and be more focused at work when you practice it often. This is what Robert L. Rosen says about self-reflection. It involves picturing yourself in the future, thinking about how you interact with others, assessing your strengths and failures, and questioning yourself about what you believe in.

You need to think about your behavior.

The value of self-reflection can never be overestimated. Self-reflection is always there to help you, whether you want to see things from a new angle or need help. It can help you get back in touch with your core values and beliefs, help you refocus, and make you take a few breaths to calm down and then go on. Looking at what makes us feel purposeful and motivated is sometimes what we need to do, rather than looking for practical ways to get things done. You can use this to do something a little different, like switch careers or change jobs. When we think about our talents and goals, we can feel better and have a better life.

Self-reflection gives you the chance to make good and beneficial changes because it allows you to think more deeply and understand more than what is on the surface. We often have a lot of different emotions, feelings, and thoughts that need to be sorted through in our heads. The good thing about self-reflection is that it lets you get back in control of things that you've let go of by accident.

Self-reflection helps you be more honest with yourself, and it helps you get rid of negative influences as you become more capable of taking corrective actions. All of this shows that self-reflection does a lot more than just making you aware and aware of your feelings, emotions, and thoughts.

It also helps you be honest with yourself about what you can do, and it makes you feel at peace with what you can't. In the past, you may have felt helpless, or like there was a lot of weight on your shoulders. You might want to remember doing some self-reflection because it can help you feel better about yourself.

You should also know that you can't control things, which can help you deal with stress.

Try to avoid these things:

In the same way, self-reflection can be very good, and it can also be very bad. The following are some things you should keep in mind:

- Don't get stressed out. Slow down when you're looking at your own life. Make an effort to only think about one thing at a time. You might feel like you have to cover everything from your identity to your ideals to your relationships to your goals and more. A single meeting doesn't have to cover everything you need to think about. Make time for other sessions to think about other things, too.

- From now on, don't pay attention to the small things. Reflecting on your positive traits is better than focusing on your successes or failures because you're more likely to be disappointed when you think about your real mistakes. You should focus on traits because you don't want to change history and improve yourself.

- Don't tell yourself lies—one of the most costly things you can do when you're thinking about yourself is telling yourself a lie. Self-reflection is a good time to be honest with yourself to get the full and proper benefits you deserve. Do not lie to yourself.

- If you're in a bad mood, don't think about yourself. When you want to do a deep analysis like self-reflection, make sure you know what kind of state you're in before you do it. Depression is a good example of a state that can be very volatile. If you think about yourself in this state, you're more likely to develop false ideas and make bad decisions.

CHAPTER 2: SEVEN CORE PRINCIPLES FOR REFLECTION

Every transformational leader must learn to think about things from time to time. Taking time to think about things can help us move forward in life, and it can also help us get more focused on our spirit. If you've already thought about what you've done this year, you should know how to start planning your new year's goals now that it's almost over. But, before you start planning, you must look back at these seven core principles because they're very important for your thoughts.

Be happy.

Reflecting on your past can help you gain energy for the future, learn, grow, and experience growth if you're positive. This is because you can choose how you reflect on your past, so it's often a good idea to choose to be positive when you're reflecting on your past. Never let the mistakes you made in the past make you feel bad about yourself. To

grow and do better, you need to see mistakes as part of life. Even if we don't succeed, we still have chances to improve, and they're experiments that assist us in reaching where we want to be. A positive attitude means that you look back at how your past has been. Even if you've had some bad experiences, think about how the lessons you've learned from them have made you a better person.

Be there.

When you stay mindful and present, you'll see things more clearly and separate yourself from your past, which will help you move forward. People call the past the "past" because there's a reason. Even though you don't want to live the past again, you can look back at it from a distance. You see, our present is a gift, and when we learn from our past, it makes our present even better and more important. Think about how you can spend more time in the now.

Be: Pay Attention

When you're thinking, it's good to be aware of what you're looking at. In this case, being wise means that you have a greater desire for intuition and understanding or for getting a better sense of things. In this way, it's a good idea to act as an objective investigator and look at your past. There is no doubt that the past few years have given you a lot of wisdom. If you peek inner, you will see that you have a lot to learn from your experiences. It's important to ask yourself questions you might be afraid to ask or questions you haven't yet asked.

Do what you say you're going to do

We can learn and develop a lot when we start with compassion in our thoughts. Reflection can help you get back on track if you've been having trouble keeping going toward your goals.

Your determination can also help you to get your goal clear. Reflection is all about learning for the present and future. You can always improve your goal and get a better picture and insight with reflection.

Become better.

The word "perfection" shouldn't make you feel bad. Even though nobody is perfect, the truth of life is that we can always work on ourselves to become better each day. There are some things we can develop from the past that can help us in the future. And even though we may not be perfect, we must keep trying to serve our friends, families, and other people better.

Remove your eye out for things that could happen.

Even though they know how important and important reflection is, many people still don't do anything to take time to reflect. Reflection helps you learn and grow, but it takes a lot of your energy, time, and focus, which are your most important things. If you spend time and energy on reflection, you'll have more to enjoy. Reflection is proactive work, and if you spend time and energy on it, you'll have more.

Be a very excited person.

Our passion is a powerful force that helps us push through our problems and setbacks and make them seem like small things. If we learn to celebrate the good things that happen to us, we'll have enough energy to keep going and keep going. In the same way, we'll be able to laugh at our mistakes and celebrate the good things that happen to us when we live from our deepest passions. Do you want to get back into some hobbies with which you've lost touch? In the last few years, what has kept you going? These are some questions you need to ask yourself when you're thinking about yourself to make it more exciting.

CHAPTER 3: QUESTIONS YOU NEED TO ASK YOURSELF.

Let's be honest with ourselves, and it can be scary when we're thinking of how we end up where we are, and we feel lost and without purpose. We risk the chances of being distanced very far from where we desire to be when we're not conscious of where we're going. Self-reflection ensures that you are fulfilled, and it can help keep you in check with your life journey. Thus, there are some important questions you must ask yourself frequently to stay en route of your path, and here they are.

1. Am I using my time wisely? The truth is that time is very important. Everyone already knows this. You can't buy time, even if you're rich or powerful. It's important to always ask yourself if your time is being used wisely because if you keep wasting your time, you're just wasting your life away. If that sounds mean, I'm sorry. It's just the truth, though. I spend my time this way: Then, what do I do with my time? If you ask someone what they do with their time, they won't say anything specific because they'll keep stammering and trying to figure out what is taking up their time. This is because they don't know what is taking up their time.

   Many users spend a lot of time "cruising and vibing" on social media. For some, gossiping is the thing that takes up their time the most. You should do things that are refreshing, relaxing, and rejuvenating. However, if you spend too much time doing things that aren't productive, you might not be healthy enough. It's also a substantial waste of time when you refuse to take the step to move from working at a place where you're not permitted to provide some sense of value, make use of your skills, or you're not challenged just because of the pay is stable. For you to see the aspect in your life that has probably been a waste of time, take time to sit and look at where you're now and imagine yourself a few years from now.

2. Am I taking anything for granted? Because we always want more, we don't see or appreciate the things that we already have, so we don't see or appreciate the good things we already have. When you think about how bad things have been in the past and not how good things are now, you're more likely not to see them.

   The lot you have. The thing is, we all have a lot of good things in our lives that we should be proud of. Every day, we have food to eat, a place to sleep, and the support of family and friends even when we think we're going to die. On the other hand, our current circumstances make it hard for us to see the good things that we have. It comes from the fact that we're always looking ahead. So, try to be grateful. Be thankful. Take a sign at what you have around you before saying something bad.

3. What perspective do I hold? Is it a healthy one or not? Our perspective is very important, and this is so because it's the underlying factor behind being successful, doing what's right, or if we're happy. Do you know that it's possible for you to feel thoroughly empty even if you have the world in your closet? The perspective in which you see things affects a lot of things, and therefore we must brace ourselves to see issues in a different light by listening to an outside perspective or stepping back. Some people are so constrained, rigid, and 100 percent about their perspective that they will never see from another perspective. When possible, learn to adopt new perspectives.

4. Am I living true to myself? Steve Maraboli once mentioned that we're not being true to ourselves if our negligence not to live in alignment is spurred by the several conflicts we have in our lives. If you demystify this saying yourself, you'll realize how weighty it is. Think of it yourself, are you living the life you want to live? Do you think you're deceiving yourself, or you're not? We must not just let things spiral away. Now and then, our circumstances and actions must be consciously evaluated. Walk away from anything you're doing that you think may Make you regret it eventually. Do well to understand the "why" behind your actions and figure out what you're doing.

5. How do I wake up in the morning? One of the massive indicators of how happy you'll be is the first thought you have for the day. It's high time you took action if you've understood why you don't always want to get out of bed and you don't like looking forward to what the day brings.

6. What do I think about before I sleep? It's different for each person. Some people think about bad things before going to sleep, while others think about good things. Last thoughts before you go to sleep can often reveal many things about your life because this is when your mind starts to clear up. If your thoughts before you go to sleep are usually negative, you might want to start looking at the things that make you stressed.

When it comes to my relationships, how much time and effort am I putting into them? For us to have fun living, we need relationships with other people. No one can survive alone on his or her own, and therefore we need each other. However, many of us take our relationships for granted, and as a result, they suffer serious damage. Right from the start, any relationship that wants to grow demands constant effort, but what happens when all the years of effort get thrown off in a very short time? You must strive to maintain your relationships, and you stay dedicated to that so that you don't lose different valuable individuals in your life.

Appreciate the people in your life and try to stay connected with your family and loved ones, even if you're away from them.

8. Am I taking maintenance of myself physically? To keep your mind strong and clear, you must find it dutiful to keep your body in good health. This is a popular quote of Buddha, and it expresses the importance of keeping your body in good shape and taking care of your body. As we get older, we're often faced with many challenges and an array of responsibilities that

often distract us from taking care of our bodies. However, we must be committed to taking care of ourselves because it's very important.

9. Do I stress myself out with matters, not in my control? Steve Maraboli once said that many people are often unhealthily attached to the things they cannot control, and therefore they're highly stressed, sick, and miserable. Remember we once mentioned how precious our time is? Good. One of the biggest ways people waste their time and effort is by bothering themselves over what they can't control. Your mental well- being, health, and days can be ruined when you perpetually let yourself be stressed by the things that are not within your realm of control. If you have any worries about things you can't control, work towards eliminating them.

10. Am I achieving my set goals? We all have our respective dreams, visions, and aspirations in life, but we tend to unconsciously throw away our goals due to a lack of self-awareness. We must learn to account for the how even as we have our eyes fixed on the where and what. To achieve our goals, it's pertinent that we break down the steps we must take along the line and examine them closely.

CHAPTER 4: WAYS TO FORGET AND LIVE A HAPPY LIFE

Sometimes, most of us find it difficult to let go of the past and live a happy life because we're still nursing the past, and we've yet to let go. Consequently, we're prompted to believe that only our past mistakes matter as we're often brooding and losing the ability to focus on the present. Leaving the past behind you is one of the best things you can do for yourself. What you become from now shouldn't be defined by your past events or experiences. You'll be able to achieve your goals and enjoy more success when you open up to a happier life by choosing to be positive, relishing in your happiness, and focusing on the Present Moment.

1. Let the Emotions Flow

One of the wrong things we used to do is deny our emotions. We act like our emotions don't matter, and as we continue to ignore them, they begin to hurt us and gradually taunt us. Learn to let your emotions flow. Feeling your emotions is very necessary if you want to move forward. For you to let go of the past and live a happy life, find what's best for you to let your emotions flow, whether it's by screaming into a pillow or crying till you feel calm. Always remember that it's okay to cry but be mindful of you're in charge of how you feel, and you're not your emotions, so you can choose how you feel.

2. Don't Let Difficult Thoughts Cloud Your Mind

Letting go of the past will become harder, and you'll be distracted from the positives in life when you unproductively engage in thinking negatively. Yes, it's good to express your emotions, but dwelling on them isn't healthy. You'll not enjoy your right to live a happy life, and self-sabotaging thoughts will continuously plague your mind if you give room to negative thoughts. You're also likely to find yourself in a depressed state if you're constantly all about the negative. Moving on from the past can be very strenuous if you let negative thoughts abide in you, and this is why you must brace yourself to steer your mind away from these negative thoughts whenever they cross your mind. You'll see that you'll enjoy more positive results when you start using positive thoughts to replace negative thoughts.

3. Learn from Your Experience

Your experiences are not only meant to hurt you; they also serve to help you learn and grow. You'll understand what makes you happy and even learn about yourself when you learn from an experience. Whatever experiences you might have had, take away the positives from it and hold on to that. Suppose you were fired from your job. You can think about what comes next for you and then take the next step to become a better person.

Happier. Because it was hardest to break up with your partner, A chance to look for more meaningful relationships can help you figure out what you don't want in a partner and what you should work on. Opportunities presented by our experiences help us know more about becoming happier.

4. Stop Being the Victim

It doesn't matter what happens in your life. You can choose to see yourself as a victim or as a survivor. Take note that it will be very strenuous for you to stop living in the past if you allow your thoughts to keep leading back to past traumas by having the mindset of a victim. You'll often find yourself in a state where you'll be thinking nothing will go right for you when you let your victim's feelings take control of your mind.

Remember that failing before doesn't mean that you're automatically bound to fail. You don't have to play the victim. Instead, see yourself as a survivor. If you do this, you'll be sure to feel good, and your emotional health will naturally improve as well. Being a survivor means that you accept your experiences and are ready to work and walk through them to become even better. Being a survivor also means that you choose not to be defined by your past.

5. Don't Wait for an Apology

Learn to forgive and forget. When someone offends you, don't be so particular about waiting for the person to come and apologize to you. It isn't helpful when you have this idea or mentality stuck into you because it will make you hold on tightly to the past, and secondly, it will make you hurt yourself more. You deserve a happy life, and someone else's mistakes shouldn't stop you from getting the happiness you deserve.

Whatever happened has happened. Let your focus be on you moving forward. What's even the guarantee that the person that offended you will come back to apologize to you? So, if there's no guarantee, why must you wait till eternity expecting an apology? Don't waste your time over apology expectations because it will hurt you more, and it can keep you trapped in your past.

6. Expand Your View of Yourself

How well do you know yourself? It's high time you started learning what makes you happy and getting to know who you are. Shift more time and attention to yourself. Learn and love with passion, take risks, and partake in rejuvenating activities. Don't be stupid to put yourself out there and get to know more about who you are. Learn to love who you are now, be kind to yourself, and treat yourself well. You can make yourself a nice meal, go for a solo walk in the park, take yourself out to lunch, or do anything that makes for a nice alone time.

7. Live in the Moment

Many people bother too much about what people will think of them or what will happen soon that they'll always miss out on living in the Moment. Earnestly and wisely, live in the Present Moment; don't anticipate troubles, don't worry about the future, don't mourn for the past. This is one of the wise sayings of Buddha, and it's a secret to a healthy body and mind. Whatever you're doing, make the most out of it. The Moment you're in now, bask in it. Enjoy the present. Tomorrow can wait. Let the past be the past. Focus on yourself and your doings. However, you may want to develop a mindfulness meditation practice if you're finding it difficult to live in the present.

CHAPTER 5: HOW YOU CAN LET GO OF TOXIC PEOPLE IN YOUR LIFE

You shouldn't think twice before you remove yourself from unpleasant circumstances and toxic people because it's necessary for your physical, emotional, and mental being, and it's okay for you to protect your health. Sometimes, you may not fully recognize a toxic person, which can make you feel isolated and inadequate with the degree of distress he or she creates.

A toxic person often exhibits toxic behavior, and the more you keep toxic people in your life, your ability to heal from them may be hindered. Toxic people misrepresent your worth; they'll misrepresent reality to you and run from accountability. Nevertheless, take note that you'll only give room for toxicity growth if you don't take necessary actions but allow your values to be dismissed by toxic people.

Whether the toxic person is your family member, friend, or partner, being in a toxic relationship with them will make you feel less good about who you are, you'll feel unsafe sometimes, you'll feel unheard, and it will seem as if your effort or time means nothing. There is a handful of reasons why many stay in a toxic relationship. It may be because of an unhealthy cycle of abuse, or they're partially stuck in a pattern for some people. Others who find themselves codependent try to be people-pleasers, fear conflict, resist change, have a lack of boundaries, or see

Themselves as a burden are likely to stay in a toxic relationship too. It may not be easy to let go of toxic people, but you must brace yourself up to do so, and here are four simple steps to follow to let go.

Recognize the Red Flags

You would have probably heard the word "red flag" several times but in this case, note that we're not talking about countries or any sport. Red flags simply have to do with the traits you see in a person, making them toxic. It can also be like a feeling you get or a sense of distrust or dissatisfaction. It's best if you can detect these behaviors as soon as you can, and you'll be able to know if the person is trying to manipulate you or not by evaluating the person; after you've identified the red flags

Here are some examples of red flags:

- The person may abuse you verbally and/or physically

- The person repeats the same patterns of behavior repeatedly after you give a second chance The person is the victim, and you're the villain

- The person lies outrightly about anything, even if you catch him or her red-handed

- The person gets mad when you say no and ignore your boundaries
- The person doesn't appreciate the goodness you provide while trying to be dear and care less about reciprocating
- Whenever you're around the person, you tend to feel drained or used
- The person sabotages your self-esteem and points out imperfections
- The person is selfish and puts himself or herself first.

Set Boundaries

Now that you've been able to identify the red flags, the next step you must take is to set boundaries. Setting rules for yourself is an important part of self-care, and you can leave at any time. You can set both physical boundaries and even emotional boundaries. Let go of that toxic person and set up a healthy emotional distance. Is this person even listening to you? Is he or she fulfilling your needs? Are you respected? Tell the person how you feel and don't walk on eggshells.

Do well to cut off the connection completely if the toxic person can't hear you out. However, you may first set some boundaries for this person and pull back if this individual is in your inner circle. Nevertheless, suppose you want to consider giving the person a second chance. In that case, you must do this with a lot of caution because this person is likely to replay his or her former behaviors or actions if he or she is made to believe that he/she can get away with anything.

Invest in Yourself

It is the best thing you can do for yourself. Kindness yourself should just be your main goal. You need to feel like you have a purpose, surround yourself with positive people, be motivated to accomplish, and take care of yourself. These are some of the little ways you can invest in yourself. Know that you're more than a million. You deserve to be loved, and you are worthwhile. For you to be able to let go of toxic people easily, you must have self-love.

Know When Forgiveness is Possible

The person in question may make attempts to prove his or her worth. Maybe the person suffers from insecurity due to their inflated ego, and the person has no idea of what a healthy partnership looks like; the person has some issues he or she is dealing with that makes him/her forget to be good to you or made some mistakes that make

Him/her appears horrible. If the person tends to apologize, that is a good place to start.

Now, be watchful of the person's actions. Is he or she just trying to manipulate you? Do you see changes? Are you seeing convictions that the decision to change is indeed true? Don't be swiftly deceived by the person's perceived personality or image, but you must start trusting the person again once he or she starts doing the right thing. However, even if the person shows remorse or vulnerability, ensure that growth and time have passed before you start forgiving the person.

More so, you must understand what forgiveness entails. The fact that you forgave someone doesn't mean that you have to do anything you don't want to do let the person back in, accept the same harmful behaviors from someone, or go back to the same relationship. Forgiveness doesn't mean reconciliation. It's just a simple release of anger or resentment. Proceed with caution if you must give that person a second chance, but just to be clear, you can forgive the person without welcoming him or her back into your life again. And lastly, have it registered in your mind that forgiveness is essential for you and not for that person.

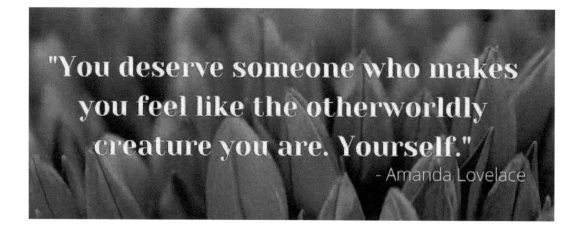

"You deserve someone who makes you feel like the otherworldly creature you are. Yourself."
- Amanda Lovelace

CHAPTER 6: THINGS YOU NEED TO DO WHEN YOU FIND IT HARD TO LET GO

Many people suffering from emotional pain are often consoled with the expression "time will heal your wound." As a result, many people have accepted that very soon; time will wipe away their fear, guilt, sadness, anger, and anguish. Nevertheless, not everyone is fortunate to find their wounds healed by time. Many people find it difficult to move on or let go at a particular point in their lives, irrespective of the fact that the passage of time is likely to ease one's pain a bit. To heal more quickly, we must do something to help ourselves because it's what we do with the time that changes us, and time itself isn't what changes us. It's time to cry. When it's hard for you to let go, crying can be very helpful. It can also help you get rid of bad chemicals in your body, which can help you get over the loss.

1. Counsel yourself to let go and move on. You need to brace yourself to let go. You can't continue living as a slave of the past. For you to let go, you must decide that you must move forward and have it registered in your mind that some people are not a part of your destiny, even if they may be a part of your history.

2. Go out with friends or family. If you're finding it difficult to let go and move on, you can find solace and comfort from your friends and family. You can gain a fresh and different perspective on things when you go out with the people you love and share how you feel with them. They'll give you the listening ears you need and help revive your energy.

3. Learn a new skill. At times, one of the reasons why you find it difficult to let go is because you're not busy. Rather than wasting time brooding over what you should let go of, get involved in the process of learning. With this, you'll even get to see new opportunities to take advantage of, you'll gain different viewpoints to explore, and you'll also grow and learn.

4. Engage in physical activity. When you find it so difficult to let go, you can engage in any form of exercise, be it yoga or aerobics. Exercise can lower symptoms related to mild depression and anxieties, improve your mood, increase self-confidence, and boost your brain's feel-good neurotransmitters.

5. Plan a Trip. Treat yourself to a scenic difference and escape from your surroundings for a month or maybe a week. Things will not become right when you confine yourself, and you can feel quite better when you change the environment.

6. Explore new paths and meet new people. You think you can't get better because you're still holding on to things you should let go of. Every day, the world is full of new things and people you can meet. You can move forward by meeting people and going out. Try to get out there and meet new people. You can join a special interest group, do community service, or join a networking group.

7. Cry it out. When you find it so difficult to let go, crying can be very helpful, and it can also serve to flush out negative chemicals in your body. Nevertheless, note that the idea isn't just to cry and keep crying. Once you're done crying, clean your face, get up, and bask in the understanding that life goes on and there are still more exciting events awaiting you.

8. Forgive. To be free to move on, you need to forgive the universe, forgive yourself, and forgive others. You cannot shrug back the need to forgive whenever you want to let go and move on because it's essential. And just as Steve Maraboli had said, you cannot move forward if you fail to see that the situation is over, forgive the situation, forgive yourself, and let go.

9. Accept the situation. Acceptance opens liberation doors to you. You'll find peace when you accept what you can't change and what has happened. When you try to change things, you'll make yourself suffer more damage and sorrow because before you can unlock the door to happiness, you must accept things as they are. You'll be able to make improvements to yourself, take control of your life, and stop hurting when you accept.

10. Use a creative outlet to express your feelings. There are diverse creative means you can explore to transform your negative emotions. Your creativity can combat the negative emotions lingering in you. From painting to blogging and vlogging, and others, find whatever is best appealing to you and use it to express or release your feelings.

CHAPTER 7: THINGS THAT WILL COME WHEN YOU START TO LET GO OF YOUR PAST

Many of us have hard times, great pain, and sadness caused by losing someone or something. It may be a relationship that we value and hope will eventually change for the better, but when the toxicity becomes more painful and causes more hurt, we must learn to let go. However, letting go has never been easy and we still often feel attached to the past because we're not sure what the future will bring. Our comfort level with the known is another thing that forbids us to bear the pain and hurt rather than let go.

For instance, if you asked someone in an abusive relationship why he or she has refused to let go, he or she would probably tell you that "the devil you know is better than the angel you don't know." This feeling of uncertainty tends to make us hold onto the past and resist change. Letting go is a hard process that takes time, but when you decide to start the journey, you'll realize that some beautiful things will start happening to you.

1. You will get to see a new positive version of yourself. We have so much power that we don't even know about humans. Though this power isn't about doing magic or making the night turn today, we do have the power to alter and define our memories, and the decisions we make also reflect the power we have. Thus, it's up to us to choose to change our future and choose what we want to spend time focusing on. This powerful new positive version of your life will be created by your memories and mind when you choose to let go of what is hurting you.

2. Make space for the new. You'll be ushered into an interesting and refreshing chapter of growth in your life, get to meet new and amazing people, get new visions, and become drawn towards new goals when you choose to let go of the past. You're forfeiting your present when you constantly replay your past. We're not purposed to live a static life because we have room for more growth, and there's a reason why life often propels us towards more growth.

3. As you face more challenges, you will deal with them with grace. What is done is done. Your past isn't meant to be an eternal punishment but a learning experience. You'll be able to easily let go and move on and even handle your next challenges without breaking a sweat if you've once been able to push through those difficulties. They say what doesn't kill you makes you stronger and wiser, and this is just it.

4. learn to love yourself first. As earlier mentioned, self-care and self-love are very important. Aside from the fact that it helps us build our self-esteem, it also makes us appreciate ourselves for who we are. When you don't love yourself, there's nothing another person can do that will make you love yourself more unless you just want to deceive yourself. Loving yourself first is the key to feeling loved, and one of the main reasons so many people stay in hurtful

relationships is because they don't love themselves, and they need to lean on another person before they can see the love. Tragic.

5. You will inspire others. How nice and good would it be to be a source of inspiration to others out there who are experiencing the same thing you've been through? You'll always feel good when you get to meet a tender, kind-hearted, and smiling souls that are in the shoes that you've once been in, and you'll always inspire them to move on too. You'll become an inspiration to many, and you'll be living proof that letting go is very much feasible.

6. You will grow dear to your destiny. Though some people may have contrary opinions, I do believe that there's a reason why we're here on earth. Life makes us stronger through all the challenges, tribulations, burdens, hardships, and experiences we've had. Have a mindset that everything you go through is designed to make you grow, and life is teaching you more with all the learning experiences you're getting.

7. You'll naturally attract what you need. When you let go of what you should, it's natural that the things you need and deserve will get attracted to you. For example, if you're in a relationship where you're abused and not appreciated, it's until you let go that you'll find someone that will treat you better. Have faith that what you request will come to you when the time is right.

8. You'll get to see for yourself that all you need is YOU. You can't lose something you are, but you may lose something you have. When you let go, you'll get to understand that you've always been sufficient for yourself. Yes, it's good to be in a loving, supportive, and blissful relationship but think of others that are not in a relationship. Do you think they're not happy? Love and attachment are two different things, and you'll be able to build an independent life and find joy in your interests and who you are when you let go.

CHAPTER 8: 15 EXAMINE WAYS TO START WORKING ON SELF- IMPROVEMENT

Self-reflection gives birth to self-improvement. Once you've been able to reflect and move on from the past, the next step is to improve yourself. Thankfully, there are several means to improve yourself if you care about your growth. As a human, you can be even better whenever you think you are good, and because the human potential is limitless, you'll always find something about you that's worth improving. Here are some practical ways to improve yourself.

1. Read every day. You'll be exposed to more wisdom when you read more books. Affirmed to be concentrated sources of wisdom, books make you wiser and make your mind travel.

2. Learn a new language. It's a mind-opening experience when you choose to learn a new language and culture. The world is fast becoming a multicultural place and learning a language is a skill that will pay you in the long run.

3. Pick up a new hobby. Whether emotionally, mentally, or physically, you'll be able to stretch yourself in different aspects when you learn something new. From web design and wine appreciation to dancing, Italian cooking, and poetry, there's a wide array of recreational hobbies you can pick on beyond your usual favorite hobbies.

4. Take up a new course. Online courses, workshops, and seminars are examples of courses you can take. Courses serve to help you improve yourself with the new knowledge and skills you'll gain from them.

5. Create an inspirational room. When you have an inspiring and welcoming space, you'll feel inspired every day. To begin with, you can commit to investing in some comfortable furniture, buying a few nice paintings for the walls, or putting on a new coat of paint. Living in an inspirational environment is very beneficial.

6. Overcome your fears. Whether we accept it or not, we all have fears. No matter how built you are, or how strong you see yourself, there's a high chance that you'll still fear something. Fear hinders us from improving, and they tend to keep us in the same position. Whether you have a fear of risk, fear of public speaking, or fear of uncertainty, pay attention to recognizing what your fears are and take action to work on them.

7. Level up your skills. To level up your skills, you must foremost be sure of the skills you have. Once you're sure, encourage yourself to become better and stronger by leveling up. Level up your public engagement abilities if you're a public speaker, level up your writing skills if you're a writer, and the list goes on and on.

8. Wake up early. They say early to bed is early to rise. So, you already know what you should do for you to wake up early. You stand to enjoy many benefits when you cultivate the habit of waking up early. Foremost, your brain will get to switch into its active mode with

The early-morning sunlight it absorbs. Secondly, you'll be able to soak up the morning tranquility. Thirdly, you'll get to add extra time to your day. When you're up before others, you enjoy more time to spare for self- improvement, which can positively affect your quality of life and improve productivity.

9. Exercise weekly and have a routine. Exercises are very crucial for a healthy lifestyle. To prevent boredom and muscle strain, do well to mix your exercises up.

10. Start your life handbook. Many people don't even know what a life handbook is, but you need not fret over that. Your goals, values, purpose, and all the things on living your life to the fullest are the essentials in this life handbook. You can see it as a manual that helps you improve yourself consistently and live your best life.

11. Write plans for your future self. Many people might find this somewhat funny or childish, but it works. After you've learned how to improve yourself, what kind of person will you be? In the next five years coming, where will you find yourself? When you write a letter to your future self, you'll feel more aligned and dedicated to working towards that person you want to be short. So, write the letter, seal it, and start working towards it.

12. Move from your comfort zone. You'll become stagnant and unable to grow when you're too relaxed and comfortable. Do you know why this is so? This is simply because sweat and hard work precede growth, and no real growth can happen without them. Thus, make a dish you've never tried, go hiking on a trail you've never been to, or just do anything that you haven't tried out before.

13. Put someone up to a challenge. Healthy competitions do aid growth. You can compete with a friend on anything you wish to improve on; it may be a financial challenge, reading books, exercise, weight loss, or anything. Competition aids self-improvement, and it's a great way to grow. And in the long run, you and the person you competed with will enjoy the benefits of going through the process.

14. Identify your blind spots. You'll be able to discover your areas of improvement when you discover your blind spots. The things about yourself that you are unaware of are your blind spots (personal development).

15. Ask for feedback. Do you ever think why people in various businesses are always particular about getting customer feedback? It's simply because they understand the value of feedback. You'll learn to improve yourself with the additional perspective given by asking for feedback. These blind spots, which they make you see, are what you'll take note of and try to improve. People who can give their feedback objectively without bias can be your boss, colleagues, family, and friends. Acquaintances can be helpful too.

SETTING FREEDOM GOALS

INTRODUCTION

To be fully productive, you need to figure out what you want to do. That means that before you can get what you want in life, you need to figure out what you want first.

Here, goal setting comes in. Even if you set your goals in the right way, you can make it harder to reach them.

Right? Wrong!

There is, in fact, an art to writing goals. You have to write your goal in a certain way. Even if you set your goals in the right way, you can make it harder to reach them. That's right: if you set a bad goal, it will hurt your chances of success.

If, on the other hand, you write your goal in the right way, it can completely change your chances of being successful and help you to more consistently follow through on your plan.

How do you achieve a goal? This isn't just about how and what you say, but also what you say. Because there's another thing that can happen if you write your goals in the wrong way: you can achieve your goals and then not be happy with what you've done.

In this book, we'll look at how you can write the right goals and then follow through on them. You'll learn about:

You need to know your life's goal and what you want to achieve. You also need to know how to write your "mission statement," How do you want to live your life? This is a statement that sums it up.

The power of imaging and how well it helps you gain what you want by making you see it. How to get even more likely to get what you want What to do after you have set goals and met them.

Here, you'll discover how to look for your own life, presume about what modifications you want, and then work on making them happen. You'll be able to be exactly who you want to be and live the way you want to live. All of this will make sense when you've done it.

CHAPTER 1: SETTING AND PLAN GOALS THAT YOU WILL BE PASSIONATE ABOUT

What we hear most often is, "Don't give up on your goals." It doesn't matter if we read a self-help book or see a motivational poster. A lot of people say, "Live your dreams," "Chase the rainbow," "Don't give up," and so on. We've heard it a million times.

This is also a very nice phrase. True, we should keep going after the things we want. We can also achieve anything we put our minds to.

What's wrong with this? Because it doesn't work out. Most of us haven't become billion-dollar rock stars or business owners because we haven't heard about it yet.

When someone says this, they should know that it's not very helpful. They say we should keep going on our dreams. We all know that. The worst part is figuring out how to pick good dreams in the first place.

You might not know what you want to be.

What if what you want to be isn't possible? Suppose two of your goals don't work together.

Some people have a very clear goal. They have one thing that makes them truly happy. Because of this, it is much easier for them to stay committed and dedicated to the project.

In this case, you might think of someone who has always wanted to become a professional athlete, so they spend all of their free time working out to be the best they can be.

Another person might be someone who has always wanted to be a chiropractor, a marine biologist, or something else.

They can start working on their goals right away and finish them to the end, no matter what.

You might not be so excited about one job. What should you do if you want to be an athlete and wear a suit? In that case, how would you deal with not having enough to do?

Then, what if you want to be an astronaut, but you want to be an astronaut when you're 40, and there's very little chance that that will happen right now?

Make a Mission Statement.

Find out what your absolute favorite is. You want to do two things. One of them is not the same as your goal, but it is important because it will help you think about your goal.

That means that some people will have a hard time coming up with a single goal. Answer: "I want to be... or achieve. "

However, knowing what is important to you and your passions can help you determine what you can do and how to do it.

This is very much like the idea of a "mission statement" in business. Short words or sentences that describe the goal of a business are called missions statements in business. These statements are called "mission statements." This will make the company's brand, tie its products together, and help them decide what to do next.

The mission statement doesn't say what the company does but why it does it, so that's what it says. It is not the mission statement's goal to make much money by selling computers. Instead, it is to help people make more by giving them beautiful tools to use. That second statement is a lot more motivating, and it helps the company figure out what matters to them when they're making products or figuring out how to market them.

Microsoft's main goal is to help people.

"To help individuals and businesses all over the world reach their full potential."

Nike's is that: To bring inspiration and new ideas to every athlete. People go to Starbucks to get coffee. People, cups, and neighborhoods are all important parts of this goal.

They go beyond the products and help companies answer real questions and build a brand that people can believe in.

Many people think Apple has lost its way and stopped coming up with new things in recent years. We might figure out why if we look at the mission statement quickly.

We used to say that our goal was to help people.

"To help the world by making tools for the mind that help people."

Inspiring: A great mission statement gives the company a real sense of direction and goal. It says today's goal is to help people.

"Apple makes Macs, which are the best personal computers in the world." "Apple is the leader of the digital music revolution because it makes iPods and sells music through iTunes."

A bad mission statement like that doesn't leave much room for interpretation or vision, so it doesn't make sense.

This is not a mission statement. It's a statement of what you want to do. And that's what you need to look at on a personal level, too, to see the difference.

It's better to say this:

"I want to be a very wealthy businessman," I say Instead of saying, "I want to do this," say:

"I want to have the power and authority to make a difference in the world in a meaningful way." Or:

"I want the money and prestige that come with using my skills at work." Maybe:

"I want to share my unique way of thinking about management with a company that truly cares about me."

It's all a little different, but they all get you closer to what makes you happy.

Make your statement and stay true to yourself with these tips!

What do you want to do with your life? Think in terms of bigger, more abstract goals. How does being an astronaut make you feel excited? Is it going to new places? Does it come from a real love of science and the universe? Is it the risk?

Once you know the core emotion or drive behind your goal, you can start writing a statement that allows people to think about it differently.

In this case, the mission statement you write down might say:

"To be a true pioneer and go to new places, both physically and in your head." Or:

"To find out the beautiful secrets of our universe." Or:

I want to live a life full of unknown danger, excitement, and thrills.

Or:

When I think of space, I'm filled with awe and wonder.

It helps you reach your goal of becoming an expert in this field, showing you how to do it in other ways. If you're too old to become an astronaut, perhaps you might work as a neuroscientist instead? So, maybe you could go out and find new things. For a documentary, maybe you could take pictures of weird animals. Maybe you could write a book about space. I think that would be interesting. It could also be possible to become an astrophotographer.

These have the same basic needs and goals, but they say it differently. Now that you know how to make a good goal, you can start.

It is, in fact, very easy to do. That fits with your way of life and your money. Important things to note

Doing this might lead you to go to some weird places, so pay attention to where you end up. Your future job might not be what you thought it would be, and you might be afraid that people will question your choices.

There's a chance that your mission statement is too big for you. Maybe it isn't big enough. I don't know. People might laugh at you, or they might look down their noses at you.

That's good because you're going about it the right way. Think about the people who have done the best and are the best at what they do. They were all revolutionaries, but not all of them. It was a group of people who were willing to change how things worked.

Everything else in this book will fall apart if you set a goal because you think that's what you should want. The right goal and vision will make you want to work hard from the inside out. When you talk about what you love, you'll be excited and charismatic, which will make others want to follow your lead.

When you want to be a flag reference, you have to be excited about your job. Why do people get up so early to train?

To make your mom happy and give you more money than your neighbor, becoming a lawyer doesn't work. Be true and honest to yourself.

People should understand that they don't need to set goals for their jobs. Having a goal for your free time is fine.

This is often a better way to develop a mission statement and a goal than just writing them down. You can take pictures of the sky in your free time if you're into that kind of thing.

Even though you've always just wanted to be a professional musician, now you just want to continue sharing your audio with the world; why not start a YouTube channel? At least, you're living the dream at least.

The more you think about what you should be doing instead of what you want to do, the less likely you will reach your goals.

In many cases, the secret to real success is to work less so that you have more time and space to do what you love. Later in this book, we'll talk about "lifestyle design," which we will talk about now.

CHAPTER 2: PRIORITIZING AND SETTING YOUR GOAL

If you want to do something, come up with a picture or idea in your head of what you want to do. Now, it's time to start making things in order and setting goals.

And this is where a lot of people will go wrong again. The difficulty is that we don't know how to write aspirations that we can achieve. Instead, we end up with unrealistic or vague goals that we can't achieve.

You can achieve some goals, but not all of them. This is the advantage between goals and visions.

All you need to do is always put down your goals and vision. But if you leave it at that, there's a good chance that you won't follow through with your plan. This is based on research that shows us this.

People who set goals say that they can almost rest on their laurels. It's hard to set goals.

But the goals that people write aren't much better.

We can say, for example, that you want to look and feel great in the short term. Be in the nice shape of your life and be healthy and happy because of it.

So you set a goal:

To lose 10 pounds by next year.

That sounds like a good goal that would work well, but I think it is way too vague and long-term for what I want to do.

People who say they want to lose 10 pounds have no idea how to get there. Because a year is a long time, you might decide to put off your training until after then.

If you don't have a lot of energy or motivation one day, you might not be able to get up and do things. One day won't make any difference, so you say to yourself, "I'll make it up tomorrow," or "I'll make it up next week." You then think that you don't have to worry about skipping your workout today because you want to lose weight over a long time.

What does happen now? So often end up trying to do all your training in a short amount of time because you've put it off so many times. A pound has been added to your weight because you've made many excuses not to work out.

Hurry now.

But then, life gets in the way.

You might get sick, be very busy, or your routine changes, and you no longer have time to train. You're now even further behind.

By the end, you realize that you won't be able to reach your goal in time, and you're very discouraged. You give up on your goal altogether.

Because this goal was:

Too long term Too unstructured Too far out of your hands

So let's think of a new goal.

This time, we want to work out for at least 15 minutes, four times a week.

Now, that goal is easier to understand and follow through on, and it's all up to you.

If you lose weight is partly because of your genes and partly because of how quickly your body burns fat. That is true, though. Everybody has 15 minutes in the day that they can use. This is all up to your drive, willpower, and determination, which means this is all up to you. This is completely up to you.

Better still, it is done right away. **Pass or fail:**

To say, "Next week I'll do better," you have already failed your goal on that week. Isn't this a simple goal? Either you do it, or you don't. If you lose, you can try again next week and not be too down about it.

Almost is true for any other goal, not just getting fit. So instead of setting a goal to write a best-selling book, set a goal to write 1 page a night.

Focusing on these smaller goals will help your big picture take care of itself. It's up to the bigger picture to grow on its own.

Then, set three goals and go after them.

The key is to figure out which small steps will help you reach your bigger goals and visions. How do you break down your goal into small steps that you can achieve?

This means coming up with a plan and making a map.

Now that you know what you want to do, you need to ensure that everything you do in life will help you achieve that goal.

As long as you work a job that you don't like at the moment, that job should be helping you get closer to the life that you want to lead. This should be in your plan.

In this way, you can figure out how to get there. You can also look at the steps you'll be taking on the way there.

Think about how you can get the goal done and what reserves you have, so stop these in mind.

Keep in mind that you can do the things you want to. Getting from where you're now and going somewhere else is the first step.

People have already said that you can be a successful musician by setting up a YouTube account to show off your music. You might not think this is the best way to reach your goal, but it will work just as well.

To get what you want, think of ways that play to your strengths. Stallone is a great person to look at for this because they did this. Stallone's dream was to be an actor in Hollywood movies, but no one gave him a chance. She didn't like his slurred speech and toned body.

He had to find a similar way to act, so he came up with this.

He did this to write a script for a movie (he was a great screenwriter). People who made movies and studios wanted to buy the rights to Rocky so much that they gave him a lot of money.

But Stallone said he would only let them have the rights to play Rocky in the movie. The studios didn't want to do it at first, but eventually, they agreed. The rest is history!

On the other hand, Arnold Schwarzenegger took a very unusual path in his career. First, he became famous as a bodybuilder, then used that platform to become a movie star and then a politician.

There are many things you know how to do and people you know. You've already made some progress. So think about the best way to reach your goals and work toward them.

Three goals to choose from

Then, look at your big-picture vision and your mission statement. Then, think about what small changes you need to make in your life to get a little closer to making that happen. Is there anything that needs to change, and how do you need to change it? Is it possible to start with something small like rearranging your home office? Getting in shape? Or looking for a new job?

Make this the first step.

Make these simple goals you can work on every day. For example, these short-term, pass-fail goals should be in your hands.

Find a new job? That isn't a goal in and of itself because it's a lot out of your control and can be disappointing.

The goal should be to send three applications per week instead of one per day. This is now completely in your hands, and you can do much better at following through on it. Again, you'll find that the "job part" will come along if you focus on this small step.

You can write down three of these steps or goals. Do that now. Three is a good number to start with because it will make a real difference in your life but won't require too much time or effort.

Guarantee yourself that these goals will happen.

CHAPTER 3: STAYING COMMITTED

So, maybe your goal is to become a very successful, confident, and beautiful person. A lofty goal, but one that can be reached if you break down the abstract concepts into steps that are more tangible and concrete.

Those might be your three main goals in this case:

The goal is to work out four times a week. Each month, you'll add one impressive thing to your CV. You'll also refresh your wardrobe with one new piece each week.

These three changes will make you more confident, improve how you look in person, and help you make more improvements in your relationships and your job.

You write down your goals, and you feel great about them because you did.

...then real life starts.

A lot of work will happen next week, but it will also be the best. Put another way: You don't think you have the willpower to look for more work experience outside of the office or take on more responsibility and training at your job. Take the waves.

People who work out four times a weekend coming home from work are so tired that they can't do it.

Because you also have no money for new clothes and don't want to spend it. You can't go shopping when you get home because it's dark.

And so you try to reach your goals a little bit but then give up on them—many times in the past. I have decided to begin a new exercise regimen on numerous occasions, only to find that it does not work for more than a week. To start a new training regime didn't work out for more than a week. Most of the time, you'll even have paid for a professional training program and still not be able to keep going with it because it doesn't work for you well enough.

After a few weeks, how many of us get tired of our new clothes? Do you keep telling yourself you'll find a job?

Another question for us then is how we can make the goal happen. Keep your goal in mind every single day. For something to work, it needs to be passionate.

The first step is to ensure that what you want to accomplish is what you want to do.

The rest of this plan will only work if this is done first.

Why? Because when you have a passion, you become more than just someone who works. The people who have passion are thought to be more attractive than those who don't have it. How would you explain your personality as a result of this?

This is one of the ways that people show how charismatic they are: They move their arms and legs. As soon as someone walks around a lot and makes big gestures while they talk to us, we think this is a sign of charisma, and we become more likely to pay attention to them, be inspired by what they say, and ultimately agree with them their point of view.

If you're gay, you'll find this very attractive.

How would you describe passionate people? They are exciting, they're driven, wired up, and they're filled with good energy.

Everyone else is drawn to you like moths when they see a bright light inside you that you turn on every day when you wake up.

Then, too, it's what will make you want to work hard.

It's simple, says Will Smith: He's willing to stay on the treadmill longer than anyone else.

Without question, Dwayne "The Rock" Johnson is one of the most brilliant men on the globe right now. He was recently awarded the world's sexiest guy. He's made a lot of money and is one of the highest-grossing actors. He has also done well in sports and acting, and there is a rumor that he's thinking about going into politics. Social media campaigns run by him are also a lot bigger than most.

There are two ways: One way to find out more about him is to look at his Instagram account. He will post every morning that he is going to the gym. It's dark outside when he works out at his gym, and his phone alarm goes off at 4 am in his pictures.

In other phrases, this is somebody serious about achieving his or her goals. His physique bears witness to this.

What time does he get up and go to the gym?

Because he loves what he does, he has faith in what he does. It's what he does.

If you can't keep up with your goals, then there's a good chance that you don't want to do them. Maybe you're going in the wrong direction.

You'll be pleased to spend a ton of money on your career, work out more, spend money on clothing, write a book, save for a trip around the globe, and more if you enjoy what you do.

How to Activate and Accept Your Desires

There's also a neurological reason why this is the way it is. When we think something is very important, our bodies go into a different state. Heart rate rises, our brain releases more dopamine and adrenaline, and we become more stressed. We become more focused, more alert, and more focused. We also become more driven.

People get this way when they're trying to fight a lion, talk to a person of the opposite sex, debate with a rival, or work on their passions.

However, when you are doing something that your body doesn't think is important for you to live or be able to thrive, your brain goes into "rest and digest." Your heart rate slows down because you make less dopamine, less adrenaline, and less adrenaline.

You become bored.

ADHD is caused by low dopamine, which means that the children and adults with the condition aren't excited enough by what's happening around them. They don't think it's important or interesting, so they get distracted by other things and act out. This is why they don't like it.

When it comes to whether this is a full-blown condition, it's hard to say! It could also be a sign of how smart you are.

In other words, the point is that if you're not focusing on your goals, you might not be excited about them.

You might need to go to the gym and do a workout today, even though it's cold outside. That's hard to do, and many people will just turn off their alarm, rollover, and pull the duvet over their heads!

To avoid this, you're going to do instead to keep your eye on the goal and try to get that important emotional drive. This is what you should do: picture it and then link it to what you're going to do. Remember why your short-term goal is just a step toward the things you want most in the world.

So now you're going to lay in bed and picture yourself looking great. It would be great to have flat, strong abs.

What would be great about having big arms if you're a women love guy? You can picture yourself filling out a lot of suits in your mind. Isn't it going to make you feel so much more confident in your body language and how you walk? Take time to think about how much more energy your body will have when you get healthy. How great would it be to come home at the end of the day and feel great?

Feel and picture the thing that makes you happy. You'll then find that you almost can't stay in bed.

If you're writing a book, try to think about what that will be like. The top of your book should have your name in big letters. Think about how it would be to have interviews. I can't believe how much money I could make. Imagine how it will change your way of life. Then, write the chapter that you need to.

Humans are thought to be unique because they can see and plan, which will allow us to make long-term plans and do even more amazing things.

A rodent might come to mind when you think about this. A mouse only does things that will help it in the short term. There is an evolutionary reason why mice want to be high-ranking, hungry, and safe. Thus, they will go where there is food. In time, they will move away from danger. And that's about it.

But humans can think about things differently. To think about. To think and to plan. That means that we can develop a way to be much happier, much richer, and much more important, and we can do that.

Still, it serves the same purpose, and the hormonal controls are still the same, so it does the same thing. Sometimes it's so difficult to keep going when things get tough. They can help you keep going. It's better not to make this mistake. If you do that, you'll do what makes you happy in the least amount of time. Sitting down and eating cake is what most people do.

Tricks: More

If you're having trouble remembering your goal, you can do one more thing to use a real-life sign. Keep things that make you happy around.

That means, for example, that you can keep a picture of someone who looks like you on hand. Then, you can read books about very successful people (more on this in a moment), or you can keep a picture of you when you were happy on your desk. Keep that idea in the forefront of your mind, and you'll be more likely to get up and go!

More ways to stay committed.

Sometimes it's so difficult to keep going when things get tough. They can help you keep going.

One of the best is something that comes from Jerry Seinfeld...

People know Jerry Seinfeld because he is a well-known writer and comedian. He has had so much achievement over the years. It doesn't matter if you like his comedy or not. He's been producing a lot of good material for a long time, and it's clear that he works very hard and is very self-disciplined.

As it turns out, Seinfeld's self-discipline isn't a fluke either, but something he's made with a specific and effective method. Brad Isaac, a software developer, learned Seinfeld's secret to self-discipline from the show. Isaac wanted to know how to keep coming up with good material for his stand-up show. He asked Seinfeld for help, and this is where the world first learned about his plan.

Do not cut the chain.

He told Isaac that his ability to keep coming up with high-quality material was just a simple result of his desire to keep coming up with material in general, which made him keep coming up with material. Writing is a good way to get new ideas. As long as you keep writing, you should keep up with many projects. You had to write every day, no matter how good your work was that day or how much work you got done on any given project.

Seinfeld also uses a calendar to make sure he writes every day, which is simple.

People who write get to put a red cross on the calendar on days when they do. This is the simple rule. Write about the days when you don't. There are two or three days where you make a chain of crosses. That makes you happy because it tells everyone else about how much effort you've put into this project while hanging on your wall.

If you don't write, you don't get to draw the "x," and the chain breaks. That way, a month's worth of work can go down the drain right away, and you feel bad about it.

This one little trick can be enough to keep you going through all kinds of tasks, from writing comedy to working out, even if you don't want to do them. As long as you don't break the chain, the desire to keep going will push you even when you don't feel like it.

How it is used and why

You can read about many different ways to be more disciplined in other self-help books. This strategy shares a lot with several of them.

"Perhaps a little daily" has been there for a long period. Self-help author Tim Ferris talks about how he sets a low goal of writing two lines every day when he's writing a book. Many people find it hard not to keep going and do more once they start working, even just a little.

So when you're trying to work out for 15 minutes, you can talk yourself into it by trying to do just 5 minutes at first. I think it's better than not doing anything at all, and once you've done five minutes, you'll find that you end up doing fifteen.

Another reason this strategy works so well is because it gives you positive feedback, making you think positively of work and reward. There is enough dopamine in the brain even though it's just across on a page. This makes it feel good to be done with something.

Finally, the strategy works well because it focuses on long-term goals, demotivating. People who try to lose "x" pounds and then don't see a change don't feel like they failed. Instead, they build a long chain and see clear progress toward their goal. With a long enough chain, your other goals will fall into place.

To get through and feel better about yourself, you can do 20 press-ups. A cross can now go on your chain. It won't be very hard to do. You can do it.

All kinds of goals can be met with this system. You get across for every day you don't smoke, and it can also work the other way around. So why not give it a try? What if one day you were in a popular romantic comedy of your own? Individuals never know.

CHAPTER 4: THE VALUE OF ACCOUNTABILITY AND USING THE ASSIST OF OTHERS

Here, we briefly talked about Tim Ferriss. He's someone we should listen to when we're setting goals and making them happen.

There is a book by Tim Ferriss called The Four-Hour Workweek. It shows people how to design life so that they only work four hours a week. Another way they do this is by setting goals and meeting them, and one of the things that Tim suggests to help them do this is to make them accountable and make them pay.

You set a goal for yourself that you can either meet or not meet every day, week, or month, and then you tell someone about it. For example, you might say that you plan to visit a new country at least once a month.

It's very easy not to follow through with a goal like that, so you're going to hold yourself accountable. How? That friend will punish you if they don't check up on you.

Tim Ferriss says that the best punishment is to die. You're going to get a lot of money from them for a good cause. The surprise? There is a satisfactory chance that they will give your money to a charity that you don't like. That way, you don't even get the feeling that you did well. This way, you've lost money, hurt your good name, and do something bad for the world.

Many people don't like this, but you're again putting the motivation for your actions in front of you by setting stakes like this. This will put your brain in a more focused, driven, and ambitious state. This is very important to you, and you're telling your body that. You're going to feel "eustress" (positive stress) as a result, which will help you work harder to reach your goal.

Whether or not you should:

We should follow this advice, but it goes against another piece of research that says it can be bad for us to share our goals.

Everyone knows that we want to stop smoking, become rich by saving money or move somewhere else. We tell people these things when we tell them about our goals and dreams.

This is a great time because everyone will be happy and excited for us. For a split second, it feels like it's already happened. You've said it out loud, and now it's a part of who you are.

But this is the real problem. It's because by doing that, you've let go of some of the mental drives to get out there and do it. You've already said that you want to do this, that it's part of your personality, and that you've already been praised for it.

You now have less motivation.

Worse, some people might say it can't be done or talk you out of your goals. It's dangerous to talk about your dreams this way.

So, for this reason, you should only share your goals with a few people, and only the individual who can help you be accountable and have consequences.

Take a chance on the fear.

That's not all. There are already consequences for not meeting any goal.

Putting your life at risk: You could live the same life for the rest of your life, with no progress or improvement.

If that sounds like a good deal, it isn't. This is the scariest idea of all because it's very real.

If you don't try to get a new job, travel while you're young, get in shape, or difference how you feel about yourself, you won't be able to do these things.

It doesn't matter if you work from 9 to 5 every single day. If you don't do well, get a reward, or have an adventure, you won't be happy. A lot of your life will go by before your death, and you'll look back and think that you didn't do very much of it.

You haven't lived the dreams you had.

You're never too old to be the person you've always wanted to be, no matter how old you are. If you follow the strategy we've talked about, there are always ways to live your dreams right now. It doesn't matter if that means paying for your seat on Virgin Galactic or if you have to play "old lady 7" in TV shows. There are some downsides to getting old, though. For one thing, you won't be able to enjoy your accomplishments as long as you did before.

So don't be late. You can't afford to wait. I hope this will help you feel the urgency and focus as well.

Getting People to Do Something

Finally, know that you can often get things done better when working with others to help you. Another reason to tell people about your dreams:

Finding a training partner is the most obvious and simple example of this kind of thing. A work-out buddy will make it even easier to stay on track with your goal of getting in shape because they'll cheer you on and help you keep going.

And motivation to go to the gym, too. You'll want to train even harder to impress them, and you won't want to skip classes because that would be letting them down.

You may do the same thing if you wish to lose weight. Keep in mind that if your partner can assist you, you'll have much better results.

You can also start a movement or group of people by yourself. If you want to start a band or a new business, you'll have to find people who are as excited and passionate about it as you are.

Otherwise, you might start a movement or a group about something else instead of this one thing. What about a weight-loss group, then? If not, what about a political group?

It might be fun to start a well-dressed club. Then, you could try to work on your projects with other people who are also entrepreneurs.

To grow and do more amazing things than you could ever do on your own, you need to be part of a movement that everyone is passionate about and driven about. This makes the movement self-sustaining and contagious, and that can help you grow and do more amazing things than you could on your own.

CHAPTER 5: MAKING THE LIFESTYLE TRANSITION

One of the things we've talked about a little bit is how a goal can change your life, but we should talk about it a little more.

Often, the adage "be careful what you ask for" comes into play here. People often set goals that don't work out the way they want.

All too often, the real work that goes into being a CEO, a rock star, or a stay-at-home mom isn't what we thought it was.

It doesn't even matter if that's not the case. Even if you don't have a big, important goal, having one will always change your lifestyle, and it's always going to be hard to adapt at first.

Lifestyle design comes in at this point, and that's how it works. It's about how you live your life.

To put it another way, you're changing your way of life so that it fits your wants and makes you happy.

All too often, we let our jobs rule our whole lives. In other words, our wealth comes from the money we make at work. There is a place we live where our job is. And we fit our "free time" into our work hours.

Work is the only thing that makes us happy, so our happiness is completely controlled. I'm about to tell you that this isn't how your life should be.

This is where lifestyle design comes in. It means working backward, which is how you do it. Before you choose a job, think about the kind of existence you want to influence. Look for a job that will help you get there.

The best way to show this is to show how you work online. The best thing about working from home is that it doesn't matter where in the world you are. You have absolute control over when or where visitors work. You have complete control over who and when you work. You can also perform whatever job you choose... You can also perform whatever job you choose. You can also do any job that you want to. This is full liberty.

After this, it's up to you how long you work to make the money you need. Do what you want with the rest of your time!

In that case, what will happen?

The best answer might shock you. It could be that you would be better off collecting dustbins. In the evening, you'll be able to spend a lot of time alone.

Working as a teacher might be the answer if you want to be a family man or woman. That way, you'll come home about when school ends, and you'll be able to spend the holidays with your kids.

To go on vacation, find a job that sends you around the world or lets you work from home.

It can also mean other things. Then, you may be able to save time by moving closer to work. The move might be so you can spend more time with your friends.

It's easy: think about what you want in life and then make the changes to help you get there. Stop letting work decide who you are and how you spend your time. Not unless you love your job so much that it drives you to do it.

CHAPTER 6: INVEST IN YOU

If you had ever wanted to do something but thought it was too hard for you?

Maybe you want to make more money, but you don't think you have the skills to apply for the job that's right for you at work.

You should not be made to feel that way.

The truth is, you can often end up taking on too much.

If you've not learned how to do it yet, you might not be able to perform it right now.

And it is at this point investing in yourself is the finest thing you can do for yourself. It makes no difference how much time or money you devote to yourself. The only way to obtain what you want and move ahead is to invest in yourself.

To be willing to work online in the manner that you desire? Then you should learn how to code.

There are instances when I feel like I'm not considered legitimate in my office. Then perhaps you should alter your appearance.

People don't seem to treat you the way you want them to. Then, think about how you interact with other people. To be more persuasive, you might want to learn how to act better or act better.

The greatest importance is to keep going.

One of your three goals might be learning X or looking better with the Y method. In the same way, you think about the "law of attraction," this will also come into play.

Individuals see you will start changing when you invest in yourself and how you talk and stand. And after you've done that, it'll be a lot easier for you to go after the things you desire right immediately!

Reading can be very powerful.

The good news is that there is just so much good information out there that can help you grow these days. There are also a lot of books that talk about these things.

There are many different ways to think about success and goal setting, but these all help you think about them in a bigger way. Many of these questions the idea that we need to find a job and work ourselves to death to try and get ahead linearly.

Reading this is important. These kinds of books not only help you learn new skills and new ways to get what you want, but they also help you keep going. How successful people think and act makes it easier for you to make that part of yourself.

To get you started, I've included a couple of my favorite novels below. A wonderful place to start is with great novels.

To work less and do more in less time, Tim Ferriss wrote The 4-Hour Workweek, a book about how to do that.

This book teaches us how to get more done in less time. If you read this, you'll find out how to get rid of distractions and focus on what you want to get done. People who go to this class will also learn how to use lifestyle design in their daily lives.

Tony Robbins wrote a book called Awaken the Giant Within How to Take Immediate Control of Your Mental, Emotional, Physical, and Financial Life. It talks about how to do this, too. If you want to change your mental attitude and see how those changes everything else in your life, this book is for you. It's a long title, but this book is a great guide. He is one of the best, and he will show you how to appreciate what you have while also being more effective at getting more.

In just 59 seconds, Richard Wiseman talks about how to think about a little change and how it can make a lot of difference.

Look at some of the most common self-help tips in this book and see if they are true. It will change how you think about changing your lifestyle.

Try to picture life as a movie. This is how you should be concerned about it. They are not aliens or martial artists. They are a lack of funds or a lack of time. They say it can't be done.

It's also a chance to learn from your mistakes, get stronger, and come back and kick ass.

The more difficult the task. The more impossible the odds are. The more ass you can kick, the better. The more triumphant your victory will be when it comes.

When you have a setback, there are two ways that you can deal with it. Give up and let it win. You can get tougher and come back to win. The choice is yours. People don't have a third choice.

Do you want to stop? Or would you like them to improve and succeed? Only when people give up do you fail. Energy Planning and Management

However, while dealing with these issues, being strategic might be beneficial. People often fail to reach any goal because they don't manage their energy well enough.

It takes a lot of time to reach a goal. To get your workouts done after work, you only have so much free time in the evenings.

Instead of dealing with time, it's not the real problem here.

The challenge of time isn't as bad as the energy challenge, but both are important.

Many trashy TVs might be because you have a lot of time. However, if you get home from work and you're worn out, you won't be able to write or train or build your business.

So, think about this and be careful with your energy. Remove other schedule components to give yourself the time and space you need to complete tasks (this might mean socializing less or canceling a weekly class). People do this by sleeping more. Get a washing machine to help you with a lot of the labor at home. Cordyceps Leaf extract might be a complementary tool for this.

No matter what, make modest adjustments. Address the problem that is causing you difficulty and alter your routine to assist you in achieving your goals.

If you can't commit to 15 minutes of exercise every day, start with 5 minutes.

Because it's better to set a tiny goal and stay to it than to set a big goal and then fail to achieve it!

CHAPTER 7: THE CONCLUSION AND MAKING YOUR ACTION PLAN

At this point, you know more about how to write a well-structured goal than most people do. You know why many goals don't work, and you know how to make your life work for you instead of against you.

That theory is now ready for use. What do you need to do now to start building your goals and sticking with them?

Step 1: Have a goal in mind.

First, think about what you want. Your ideal future looks like this. This is how you envision your life. Don't be concerned if you can't think of it.

The second time things go wrong comes later on. When you've been living that way for a long time, it's when you've started to get tired of it and when you've just lost your desire to do it. You might have forgotten about your move to change by the third year. You might have been distracted by other things in your life and not remember your move. It's easy to get lost this way.

Consider what has made you happy in the past, or observe other individuals living the life you desire. This is how you envision your life. Don't be concerned if you can't think of it.

Consider what has made you happy in the past, or observe other individuals living the life you desire.

A mission statement is the second step.

Take this vision and put it into words as a mission statement. What are the most important parts of this vision? What is the emotion that makes you want to achieve that?

Step 3: Make a Plan.

Make a plan now to make that happen. In other words, you're going to think about how you can meet your mission statement in the best way possible, given your situation. This doesn't have to be about your job!

The fourth step is to set goals.

Here are your goals. These are the small steps you can take every day to reach your goal.

Don't break the chain!

Give yourself a tick every time you reach your goal to keep the chain going. If you are having a hard time motivating yourself, think about the vision and connect it back to that in your mind. If something doesn't work, pay attention to that as well!

People can help you with Step 5.

Tell a few people and ask them to make them real to ensure you don't just give up on your goals. Look for other people who can help you by joining your cause, as well!

Step 6: Help You Reach Your Goals

Look for strategies to improve your lifestyle to help you attain your goals. If you want to live a good life, you need to think about what kind of job, location, and other things you should do to help you get what you want and reach your goals.

Step 7: Check and Double-Check.

Do this all the time to make sure you are getting the most out of your goals. Address your failure points and look for ways to improve your chances of winning.

CONCLUSION

One last thing that is very important to achieving your goals is remembering to appreciate them. We forget this all too often, making the whole thing meaningless.

People do this when they work so hard to get to their goal and then their next goal that they don't stop to enjoy what they already have.

Imagine that you finally have that best-selling book out in the world. Then, you start to think about everything you didn't do right in the first book. Then you start writing your next book right away.

Your dreams have come true. You're very successful, but now you're just stressed out. Not the best. It makes it pretty easy for us to lose interest in our aim right away.

So make sure that you enjoy your accomplishments, too, and that this is part of your plans. Tony Robbins says that the best way to start each day is to think about what you've done and how that makes you feel. At the beginning of each day, think about the things you're grateful for, whether that's having a place to live or being healthy.

To keep you going, this will keep you full of energy and optimism and help you keep moving forward! The fact that you've already done so much should remind you how much more you can do.

TRANSFORM INTO YOUR IDEAL SELF IN 8 STEPS

TRANSFORM INTO YOUR IDEAL
SELF IN 8 STEPS

Are you experiencing the life of your dreams? How would one get there?

Fortunately, it's not as difficult as you may assume! You may begin living the life you desire sooner than you think by following this eight-step method.

Before you know it, you'll be living the advantages of your dream lifestyle rather than simply fantasizing about it.

FOLLOW THESE DIRECTIONS...

1. Determine your destination.

What are your objectives? How would you describe your perfect life? You cannot describe your ideal self until you know where you wish to go. Your ideal self is capable of creating the life of your dreams.

2. Identify the sort of individual who can help you achieve your objectives as rapidly as feasible.

Now that you've determined the style of life you desire consider the type of person who can make it a reality. What would it take to go from your current location to your desired location as rapidly as possible?

What sort of person would this be?

3. Define your ideal self's habits. Consider anything that comes to mind. Here are a few items to get your mind working:

How frequently does he clean his teeth every day? Is he a flosser? When does the flossing occur?

When would she go to bed, and when does she wake up? Is she a reader in bed? What is she now reading? Is she a regular reader at another time of day?

How does he begin his day?

Does she exercise? How long will it take? How frequently? What kind of exercise does she do? What does she consume? How frequently? What is her weight?

Is this true for the journal? What is the journal's subject matter? What does she think as she is stuck in traffic?

4. Describe their characteristics in detail. An individual is more than their habits. Consider some other attributes.

What is she dressed in? What kind of automobile does she drive? Hairstyle?

What are your attitudes regarding dating? Would he approach a visually appealing stranger and initiate conversation? Is it better to date a single individual or a group of people?

Is she courageous? Cautious? Calculating? Giving? Selfish? Practical?

Religious? Spiritual?

What are his morals and convictions? What abilities does she possess?

And everything else that comes to mind. Assume you're developing a character for a film. Be quite specific.

5. Incorporate the SWISH pattern.

This is a very effective approach for persuading oneself to behave following your ideal self.

Have a crystal clear mental vision of your ideal self, complete with all the habits, qualities, and features you desire. The image should consist entirely of your ideal self, with no background or context—just a blank screen with your ideal self standing in front of it and staring at you.

When you are urged to act inconsistently with your ideal self, recall that image and act correctly instead. This is a useful strategy.

6. Begin.

Consider all of the behaviors and qualities you identified. Consider incorporating a couple of the simpler ones into your life. Rep this procedure until you've lived through them all.

7. Investigate for proof.

At any point when you notice yourself acting like your ideal self, call attention to it. You may even tell yourself, "See, I am evolving into my ideal self." I am the type of person who lives only on food.

8. Maintain a journal.

Maintain a record of your progress. This will help you improve the habit of concentrating on this vital aspect of your life. Keeping track of your progress will help motivate you.

Pursuing your ideal self will provide you joy, increase your life satisfaction, and provide you with the motivation to continue on your journey. What are you doing with all of these benefits? Begin today!

HOW TO DESIGN A PLAN FOR YOUR LIFE WHAT DO YOU WANT?

Life is to be savored and enjoyed. Each person on earth deserves to have a wonderful life. However, to live a life you love, it's important to consider a Life Plan in which you've formulated everything you want out of Life.

1.   Your Home. This chapter encourages you to consider whether you're living in the place you want and the type of home you prefer. Also, setting up your home to fit your wants and needs is addressed.

2.   Career and Work. In this chapter, you'll be asked to ponder your career and ask yourself if you're getting everything out of your work that you're seeking. Also, you'll be encouraged to think about whether you're doing the type of work you want.

3.   Love Relationships and Family. What are your desires about your love relationship and family? Reflect on your current love relationship and whether your wants and needs are met in the relationship.

4.   Friends. This section covers how you feel about your friends. You'll think about whether your current choice of friends are the kind of friends you want.

5.   Health. Physical and emotional health issues are explored concerning your wants and needs. Consider any changes you want to make in these areas and include them in your plan.

6. Character. Because each person has his list of the desired character traits, this chapter asks that you consider your character traits — those you have and those you'd like to have or alter somehow. Desirable character traits can be developed and, therefore, should be written into your Life Plan.

7. Hobbies and Activities. This chapter prompts you to explore your use of spare time. As you think about the hobbies and activities you seek to do, you can make them a part of your plan for Life.

8. Intellectual and Cultural Pursuits. People vary widely in terms of what they seek intellectually and culturally. This chapter addresses these subjects and asks you to include these areas in your Life Plan if you deem them important and valuable in your own Life.

Designing your Life Plan can be an enjoyable experience. To create your plan, think about the various areas of your life: your home, work, relationships, family, friends, health, character, use of spare time, and your desire for intellectual and cultural activities. Your life will become more fulfilling when you write and follow your LifePlan!

WHY YOU MIGHT HOST A
FAREWELL PARTY FOR YOURSELF

Here's a novel thought that can assist you in becoming the finest potential version of yourself: Throw a party for yourself!

Allow me to explain.

This is not going to be a typical knee up. Rather than that, this celebration will be about bidding farewell to an old chapter of your life – perhaps an old version of yourself – and ushering in the new.

Why the Time Has Come to Say Goodbye

Too many feel "stuck" by our personalities, backgrounds, and characteristics. We might become imprisoned in what is known as "pattern thinking" or "type thinking," in which we behave in the same way we have always done... just because we have always done so.

This is for a variety of reasons. We might discuss the neurology of plasticity and how repeating certain behaviors makes them much simpler to repeat in the future (which increases our likelihood of repeating them even more!).

However, there are certainly more obvious surface reasons for this.

We have a preconceived notion of ourselves and wish to act in ways that look consistent with what we have learned about ourselves. We all believe that we are a certain way. Perhaps you are "funny," or perhaps you are someone who "does not take bullshit."

Whatever the situation, if you begin to "revert to type," it can become extremely difficult to break out of this

tendency. This is who users are; this is the behavior that everyone requires of you; how can you behave differently?

However, if that means you're going to continue endangering your health just because you've always been the person who clears his plate entirely, that may be a major mistake!

In other words, we may resort to typing when we are exhausted or weak. While you may attempt to develop new habits and behaviors, it is always simpler to revert to old ones.

However, by hosting this "going away" party for yourself, you psychologically conclude that phase of your life and that chapter. This can have a significant effect by convincing you that the time has passed and providing a compelling reason not to return. It has drawn a line across it, and you know that you cannot "go back" without incurring substantial repercussions or going against what you stated you would do.

It's time to bid farewell!

WIN ANY BATTLE

Foreword

"One is not born with bravery, but one is born with the ability to be courageous. We can't practice any other virtue consistently until we have bravery. We can't be generous, kind, truthful, compassionate, or honest." Maya Angelou's quotation

Not everyone dares to face all of life's difficulties—those who are not afraid to take risks to conquer any obstacles. Courage isn't something that everyone is born with. However, everyone has a certain degree of Courage, allowing them to face their anxieties and take chances without losing faith and attempting to live even when things are difficult.

Everybody yearns for bravery. It is a quality of character that qualifies someone for respect. This book will teach you all you need to know about cultivating bravery and using it to tackle life's obstacles. So take merit of this opportunity to learn more about bravery and the advantages of developing sufficient Courage to win any confrontation.

CHAPTER 1: KNOW YOUR STRENGTHS

Synopsis

You must have strengths to do anything or thrive in life. You might not have the guts to confront life's obstacles if you don't recognize your strengths. The things you believe you're excellent at aren't your strengths. Just because you're excellent at something doesn't imply you're strong at it. It must also be your passion for it to be your strength. It is because of this that it is considered a strength. What are some strategies for learning and honing your skills?

Ways to Learn Your Strengths

Your strengths will serve as your fuel for developing Courage. Strengths will make you feel strong. If you are confused about your strengths and weaknesses, here are some useful tips to give you a better understanding:

- write Down What You Think You Are Good at

Making a list of the things you believe you are strong at might assist you in determining your abilities. It can be your strength even if you despise doing it yet succeed at it. So, make a list of everything you excel in because it will benefit you in the long term.

- Don't Get Other People's Opinions When Learning Your Strengths.

It is not better to ask for other people's opinions when discovering your talents. Even though others have a good idea of your abilities, you are the only one who truly understands yourself. As a result, when you uncover your talents, don't allow people to influence you since your genuine strengths are hidden deep within you. That is why you, not others, should be the ones to uncover your abilities.

There are several reasons why you should not seek other people's opinions. One explanation is that someone else's perception of one of your strengths might be utterly incorrect. You will always know yourself better than anybody else, no matter how well you know them or how well they think they know you. Making a list of the things you believe you are strong at might assist you in determining your abilities. It can be your strength even if you despise doing it yet succeed at it. So, make a list of everything you excel in because it will benefit you in the long term.

- What Makes You Excited

Everyone has a source of joy in life. So, what piques your interest? One of your strengths might be your enthusiasm for anything you want to undertake. You must remember that to be a strength, and you must be passionate about what you do. It might be considered a strength if you enjoy what you do and are good at it.

- **Take Some Self-Assessment Tests**

A good way to learn your strengths is by taking some self-assessment tests. Some numerous experts and professionals offer such tests for free. You can try any self-assessment test you want. Just make sure that they will allow you to learn your strengths.

Taking these tests may be a waste of time for some but can be extremely helpful for others who are confused and don't know where to get started. Besides learning one's strengths, self-assessment tests can also allow you to determine your weaknesses, which you can improve in the long run for them to become one of your strengths. Keep in mind that some weaknesses can be the key to success at something.

Signs of Strengths

Another way to learn your strengths is to be aware of their signs, and they include:

- Success

This shows that you are effective at The activity you are doing.

- Instincts

Look for activities that you naturally enjoy. Then take advantage of them.

- Growth

When you can focus on one thing, time flies by.

- Needs

Several hobbies may exhaust you, but they will also be satisfied.

After you've identified your abilities, the following step is to develop them. Your strengths will only get stronger if you continue to nurture them. If you take it for granted, it might turn out to be a weakness in the long run.

There are different things you can do to nurture your strengths. One of the things you can do is get involved in activities to use your skills. By acquiring this, you will not just be able to learn more, but you will also have the opportunity to improve your strengths, especially if you have competitors who you think are better than you. So, don't waste time on something that will not add value to your strengths. Nurture your strengths and reap their benefits.

CHAPTER 2: THINK POSITIVELY

Synopsis

It's not simple to maintain a happy attitude. Others frequently reinforce negative thinking, especially if they are emotional and unable to manage situations well. However, they don't realize that negative thinking just serves to confuse matters and will never bring someone down the correct route. Every difficulty is the same as the one you faced in math class in school; there is always a solution, and it may be right around the corner. On the other hand, thinking positively might help you stay motivated. This will provide you with the Courage to win any battle, no matter how difficult.

When Things Go Wrong in Life, Here's How to Stay Positive

Even when your life appears to be falling apart, you must think positively to be joyful. Have you ever attempted to observe someone who is constantly cheerful and wondered how they do it? They feel special due to their positive outlook and way of life. Positive thinking may help you achieve your goals in life. This will also make your life a lot simpler.

Here are some suggestions for maintaining a cheerful attitude when things go wrong:

- Learn to live your life rather than just exist. Every day should be lived as if it were your last. It is contagious to have passion and a good view of life. If you keep a positive attitude, more people will want to be around you.

- Rather than reacting, take action. Do not wait for anything to go wrong before taking action. By being proactive, you can make things happen for yourself. If you react to your situation, things will not become any worse. It is entirely up to you to create the life you choose. You only have one chance. Receive things as they are and make the perfect of them.

- Whatever the situation's outcome, never give up hope, for everything happens for a reason. Even though it appears to be unpleasant, every circumstance contains the potential for good. Draw Your adversity has given you strength. Even if things go wrong, staying optimistic will assist you in getting through it.

- Be Appreciative of What You Have. Those who have achieved success understand that appreciation is more powerful than unhappiness. Ambition has no negative connotations. Don't forget, though, to be grateful for what you have. People who are unhappy or dissatisfied may believe that they will never achieve their goals.

- When Opportunities Come Along, Seize Them. Do not neglect your responsibility to chase your dreams or pass on the opportunities that perfectly fit your life.

- Possess a wry sense of humor. Individuals like to be around people who can laugh at themselves, even when having a bad day. Learning to grin or laugh at oneself is important for thinking positively.

- Have in mind that you are in charge of your destiny. You are the only one who can refuse your aspirations. As long as you are not dead, there remains hope. Even if you aren't accomplishing anything with your life, you have limitless potential. So, why not get right in and create the life you want?

It's difficult to keep an optimistic mindset when things aren't going well. However, it is not impossible to accomplish. Simply remember the advice given above, and you will be on the correct track.

Other Suggestions for a More Positive Mindset

Set Clear Goals is another strategy that might help you think more optimistically.

You'll never know where your path ends if you don't know what you want to achieve in life. However, if you create clear goals for yourself, you will find fulfillment. So, make a list of your objectives and adopt a positive mindset.

- Form a Mental Picture of Your Success

Forming a mental picture of your success may seem ridiculous. But, this can inspire you to achieve all your goals. You will also be motivated to reach the dreams you desire in life.

- Take Responsibility and Ownership for Your Life

Do not place blame on people or difficulties for your failures. Don't let yourself become a victim. You're the captain of your boat, and you get to determine where it goes. Make a new strategy and take action as quickly as possible if you are unhappy with your life.

- Fake Your Failures

Consider fake it if everything else fails. If you are nervous, worried, or doubtful, you can pretend that you are self-assured and confident. Smile and act as though you're a professional, successful, and positive. You can fool others and your brain. With this, you will be confident and be a positive person.

- Eliminate the Negative

Try employing positive self-talk to fight the negative ideas and uncertainties that enter your head. By thinking positively, you may overcome your fears regarding hurdles and challenges. Problems should not be overlooked. You must confront them to have the guts to do so.

Negative thinking may be a convenient alternative since it is more comfortable and offers fewer problems. Don't be caught in this trap.

CHAPTER 3: CONNECT SPIRITUALLY

Synopsis

Having the strength to tackle your life's challenges will help you stay on course despite the challenges. However, without religion, most of you may lose trust in your ability to battle. This is the primary cause for your actual Courage. You should also consider the relevance of faith. Spiritualism is the pursuit of something sacred, and it is something that people should think about. Meditation, religion, personal introspection, and yoga are ways people approach spirituality.

Why Is Spirituality Necessary to Be Courageous?

Others may not feel that spirituality has a role in the development of Courage. However, they don't realize that a successful person can never be whole without it. That is why a spiritual connection is crucial.

The methods are some of the reasons why spirituality is necessary for Courage:

Spiritual people are generous people. Psychologydemonstrates that were expressing gratitude is connected with numerous positive emotions like overall vitality, generosity with resources and time, and optimism. Spirituality also encourages everyone to be positive, which may be expressed in various life practices.

- Spiritual Individuals Are Compassionate. Experiencing compassion towards other people is one of the things that people receive from having a spiritual life. A variety of pro-social or positive emotions have strong links with spiritualism.

- Spiritual Individuals Flourish. Many say that spirituality is linked to numerous aspects of human- like. Those who are spiritual have positive relationships, are optimistic, have high self-esteem, and have purpose and meaning in life.

- Spiritual Individuals Self-Actualize. People with great spirituality aspire to live a better life. Fulfillment and personal progress are also top priorities for them. Spirituality is a term used to describe a state of they're also seen to be a route to self-actualization. This is because it forces everyone to focus on their ideas and encourages them to strive to improve as individuals.

Spiritual people take the time to savor their life experiences. Spiritual people take the time to reflect on their everyday activities and create enduring recollections of their adventures. Spiritual people learn to appreciate the tiny joys in life because they are more aware of their actions.

Some people may find it difficult to be spiritual. However, if you want to prosper in this insane world, you must have Courage and spirituality.

WIZARD OF OZ GUIDE TO BRAINS,
HEARTS & COURAGE

While Dorothy wears the magical slippers, the other Wizard of Oz characters rely on brains, hearts, and courage. See what this classic movie can teach you about developing the qualities you need to be successful and happy.

Lessons from the Scarecrow on Having Brains

Help others.
When Dorothy asks the Scarecrow why he's looking for a brain, he answers that he wants to serve others. Contributing to society is an ideal way to use your mental powers.

Solve riddles.
The Scarecrow also says he's interested in cracking mysteries. When you're stumped, analyze the situation to find a new approach.

Keep learning.
If the Scarecrow were around today, he'd probably be volunteering for on-the-job training and signing up for online university courses. Engage in life-long learning to expand your knowledge. Ask your local librarian to suggest books for you to read and find a challenging hobby to enrich your weekends.

Work smart.
Working smarter instead of harder will help you to accomplish more with greater ease. Scratch low-priority tasks off your to-do list. Master the art of delegating. Focus on your strengths and take refreshing breaks regularly.

Smile and laugh.
The Tin Man thinks he needs a heart in order to smile, but all he requires is a little oil. Loosen up so you can experience more joy and share it with others.

Be human.
The Tin Man is correct when he says having a heart makes us human. Animals follow instincts and computers operate according to their programs. As humans, we can choose thoughts and actions that align with our values.

Express compassion.
Caring about others and working to relieve their hardships makes our lives more meaningful. We deepen our friendships and experience more gratification.

Forgive others.
Pardoning others allows us to move on after we think we've been slighted. We can wish others well regardless of their actions. Forgiving ourselves also restores our peace of mind

Give generously.
Sharing our blessings multiplies them. Volunteer in your community and donate money to charity. Invite an elderly neighbor out for lunch or offer to clean out the office refrigerator.

Reassure yourself.
The Lion sounds like a wizard when he realizes that he mostly scares himself. Facing our fears teaches us that we are strong enough to overcome them.

Practice wisdom.
On the other hand, the Lion also points out that running away from danger sometimes makes sense. Our lives are too precious to waste.

Stand up for your values.
Moral courage can be just as impressive as climbing mountains. If you can be true to your convictions, however unpopular they may be at the moment, you'll lead a more authentic life.

Take risks.
Each day brings us many opportunities to triumph over our doubts. Chat with a stranger on the bus if you want to work on your conversation skills. Register for a cooking class if you've been hesitant to invite friends over for dinner

Accept discomfort.
It's easy to exaggerate the consequences when you feel uncertain about your abilities. Often, the only thing at stake is the possibility of looking a little foolish or stretching beyond your self-imposed limits. The rewards are usually worth it as you discover you're smarter, kinder, and braver than you thought.

Being well-rounded makes it easier to defeat the Wicked Witch of the West, or reach your own personal goals. Build up your heart and mind and tackle each challenge with courage!

11 QUICK WAYS TO BOUNCE BACK FROM A SETBACK

Successful people had to deal with many setbacks to get where they were. This is a critical component of success. If you give up quickly when a reversal occurs, you're unlikely to achieve real success.

Recognizing that setbacks will happen to develop a plan for coping with them is vital. A little planning goes a long way.

Consider these techniques to move ahead fast after your next setback:

1. BECOME ANGRY.

Anger isn't all harmful. Anger may be a good emotion if used to propel you ahead. A lot of things have been done with rage and contempt. Maybe this may be one of those instances.

2. BECOME DETERMINED.

A setback can be used to solidify your determination. Maybe you haven't been 100% committed, and this is your wake-up call. Are you ready to answer that call?

3. USE THE SETBACK TO BECOME STRONGER.

What can you learn from this setback? Use this situation to become better than you were before. Get what you can from the reverse and come back even stronger.

4. SPEND TIME WITH A SUPPORTIVE FRIEND.

Maybe you need some time with an uplifting friend that will give you a hug and a pep talk.

5. VIEW THE SETBACK AS A CHALLENGE.

View your setback as a puzzle to be solved. Or a test of your determination. Or a challenge for you to overcome.

6. KEEP YOUR EMOTIONS IN CHECK.

Avoid getting too emotional if those emotions will likely derail your future efforts. Anger can be helpful too. Hopelessness cannot.

Strong emotions can lead to poor decisions.

7. ACCEPT RESPONSIBILITY.

Take all of the responsibility for your setback. If you blame someone else, you lose your power to change your situation. It doesn't matter where the failure occurred. Accept the responsibility. It might not be fair, but what other choice do you have?

8. GET EXPERT ADVICE.

A setback might be a sign that it's time to call in an expert and receive some assistance. This can be accomplished with the assistance of a mentor, a counselor, or an informed friend. Get the help you deserve. However, ensure that you're receiving assistance from someone that actually can help!

9. GET A FRESH PERSPECTIVE.

It might be time to temporarily disengage and try to see your situation from a different angle. Ask someone you trust for their viewpoint on your situation.

10. DOUBLE YOUR EFFORTS.

It's possible that you need to work harder. You may have underestimated the effort or time necessary to accomplish your goal. Maybe the setback was something you should've predicted but didn't. It might be time to get severe and double down.

11. SET A NEW GOAL.

A significant setback might be a sign that it's time to set a new goal. The traditional notion is that you should never give up, yet specific goals are out of reach or demand an excessive amount of time and energy.

WHAT WILL YOU DO?

Setbacks will happen. They can be related to your goals, health, finances, relationships, career, or other aspects of life.

How you decide to handle these setbacks influences the type of life you'll live.

It's easier to deal with something if you're prepared. Consider how you would react to a significant setback in your life. How do you believe you would respond? Do you have a strategy?

Become a master at dealing with setbacks, and you'll live a successful and fulfilling life.

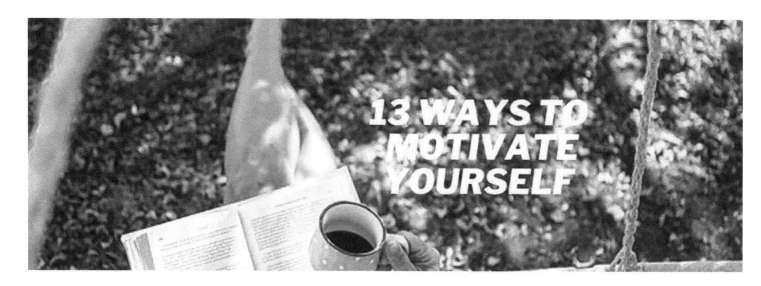

13 WAYS TO MOTIVATE YOURSELF

Motivation never seems to persist for an extended period, but that's fine. There are several strategies to reignite your motivation. Each day, begin by rekindling your motivation. If your drive starts to wane, you'll know how to restore it.

Specific individuals appear to be constantly driven. This is not a coincidental occurrence. They are born with an innate ability to inspire themselves. We can apply what we've learned to the rest of us who aren't so fortunate.

Utilize these tactics to provide yourself with an extra dose of inspiration whenever necessary...

1. MAKE A REWARD PROMISE TO YOURSELF.

Give yourself something to anticipate! It may be as straightforward as a magazine subscription or as intricate as a vacation to Thailand. Perhaps you'll reward yourself with a bit of television break if you're able to accomplish your domestic duties by a particular hour.

2. CREATE A VISION OF SUCCESS.

Visualize yourself succeeding and feel how good it feels. If you anticipate feeling good about doing something, you are more likely to complete it.

3. COMPILE A LIST OF BENEFITS.

What are the benefits of completing your task? What advantages do you enjoy? Consider how you can use logic to your advantage. Remind yourself of the benefits of the transaction.

4. COMPILE A LIST OF DISADVANTAGES.

Utilize discomfort to your advantage. What are the ramifications of failing to finish your assignment? How are you going to be harmed? What are the disadvantages? You may obtain a great deal of motivation by weighing the benefits and drawbacks of taking or not taking a particular activity.

5. REMINISCENCE YOURSELF OF YOUR PREVIOUS SUCCESSES.

If you're lacking drive due to self-doubt, consider your previous accomplishments. Increase your confidence, and you'll feel more driven.

6. BEGIN AND THE MOTIVATION WILL FOLLOW.

Sometimes you only need to go to work; motivation will follow. Begin and observe what occurs!

7. VIEW AN INSPIRATIONAL VIDEO.

Avoid the temptation to spend an excessive amount of time viewing videos, but a short, inspirational film might assist you in getting started.

8. PLAY AN INSPIRING SONG.

Put some motivational music on and go to work!

9. CONSUME INSPIRATORY QUOTES OR BOOKS.

Again, avoid squandering excessive time. A few inspiring quotations or even a chapter from an inspirational book will be enough to spark your imagination.

10. CLEAN OUT YOUR WORK AREA.

It might be challenging to maintain attention when working in a busy area. Take a few seconds to clean up. Consider using this as an excuse to thoroughly clean your property. You are not required to clean the refrigerator to work at your workstation

11. CONCENTRATE ON A FEW IMPORTANT TASKS EACH DAY. Reduce the length of your to-do list, and you'll experience less overwhelm. Overwhelming tends to reduce motivation.

12. AVOID CONCERNING IMPORTANT THINGS.

Keep your attention on the vital things, and you'll keep a higher drive level. Each important day necessitates a condensed list of activities.

13. SET SHORT-TERM GOALS.

The word "very brief" may relate to a week or 10 minutes. Whatever is comfortable for you is OK. Think how much work you can do in the next 15 minutes. If you repeat this process frequently enough during the day, you'll be shocked at how much work you can accomplish.

Avoid becoming concerned if your motivation appears to be dwindling. There are several strategies for regaining lost motivation. Motivation is transient, so it is vital to re-establish it regularly. Motivation is the fuel that propels us forward. Knowing how to produce it on demand is a very effective talent.

15 EASY WAYS TO EMPOWER YOURSELF

How big someone's bank account doesn't mean a damn thing. It doesn't even matter what title you have on your piece of paper. Is what you do important?

Should you want to be a positive experience and have a good time?

Have a better idea of who you are? See this list of 10 things you can do right now to improve your skills and confidence.

Self-empowerment: These are some of the general ideas about it.

1. This is the first step. Make goals that are the right size. People get excited about small victories. It's best if you set goals that you can reach. Cut back on sugar in your coffee until you lose 50 pounds.

2. Become better at what you do. The more you keep learning, the more chances you have to do well in your job. You can read self-help books and take online classes on communication or coding to help you improve your life. Talk to other people about what they know and teach them what you know.

3. Keep your emotions in check. People who go outside their comfort zone can be afraid. As you decide, pay attention to how you feel and think about what you want to do. decisions that will help you in the long run interests. When your emotions are intense, think about them or talk to people who can help you figure things out.

4. Trust in yourself. Challenge the assumptions that have kept you from moving forward. Think positive and think about what you can get.

5. Find people to help. Empowering yourself can improve your relationships with other people. Stay with people who make you feel good about yourself. Be honest and ask for help when you need it.

QUICK AND EASY WAYS TO POWER UP:

1. Take care of your time. Treat your time as a valuable commodity. As a way to get the most out of your time, write down the ones that you care about the most Keep away from things that could throw you off course.

2. Take care of your privacy, as well. Is there anything you do when someone asks you a question you don't like? Set healthy boundaries and be assertive when you need to keep them. Let go of the idea that you can't finish something. Conversations that make you feel bad.

3. Meditation is the third thing you should do. It would be best if you did this every day. As much as you know about yourself, it is convenient to be big and strong for yourself. Take a look at your thoughts through relaxation or other ways, like writing down your thoughts in a diary. You could also take temperament questions online and ask for help from people who know more than you do.

4. Take care of yourself. When you value yourself, you need to make sure that you care for yourself. Eat a healthy diet, exercise every day, and get at least 7 hours of sleep every night.

5. Stick to your money. People who get their finances in order will feel more secure and do more essential things. Make a plan for how you'll save, spend, and save money.

Investments. If you need more help, talk to a professional.

6. Share the housework. Does your spouse do an excellent job of taking care of things around the house, as well as taking care of kids? Begin a conversation about making some changes and keep track of your progress.

7. At work, show that you care. It may be more than good work that makes you visible at work. Keep your boss up to date on what you've done and give credit to others to build teamwork and cooperation.

8. Take care of complaints. As far as customer service and apartment management go, how do you handle things when they happen? But no need to disguise your feelings inside, so don't. Instead, say what you want and get it instead. Be tactful and direct as you fight for your rights, but don't back down.

It's essential to use positive words

9. An excellent way to deal with stress and overcome problems is to repeatedly say positive things to yourself. Visit affirmation websites, or write your own words and use them.

10. Make sure you are standing in the right way. Body language significantly impacts how you feel and how other people see you. Stand up straight and raise your head.

Take charge of your own life to enjoy more happiness and success.

Have faith in yourself and make good decisions that move you closer to your goals.

18 WAYS TO CHANGE YOUR LIFE

If you start with one action, change may be straightforward. You become happier, healthier, and more successful as each minor alteration becomes part of your daily routine.

Try a more gradual approach if you've been putting off taking action because it feels too overwhelming. Start with this list of simple resolutions, and then add your own.

1. Increase your fiber intake. Eating a high-fiber diet can help you lose weight, regulate your blood sugar, and maintain regularity. Vegetables, fruits, and whole grains are all better sources.

2. Drink plenty of water. Hydration offers you energy and promotes good skin, digestion, and cell health. Bring a water bottle with you all day so you may sip as needed.

3. Exercise regularly. Physical activity encourages you to lose weight and improves your mental and physical health. Strength, flexibility, and heart health are considered when training. You'll want to remain with your program if you can find a range of things that you love.

4. Get plenty of rest. Maintain a regular bedtime and wake-up regimen. To avoid mental stimulation and bright lights interfering with your sleep, turn off laptops and televisions at least 2 hours before bedtime.

5. Take care of your tension. Inflammation, heart disease, and other dangerous illnesses can be caused by chronic tension. Relax with a warm bath, daily meditation, and instrumental music.

6. Keep an optimistic attitude. Keep a positive attitude by concentrating on the positive aspects of life. Give yourself a pep talk and consider how you may turn setbacks into opportunities.

1. Make a lot of connections. By developing your most critical relationships and reaching out to new colleagues, you may warm up your network. Join a professional organization or go to a famous business event.

2. Continue to learn. Update your abilities and broaden your knowledge. Take online classes and see great performers at work.

3. Put on a successful outfit. Make a better first impression with your look. Visit a salon for hair and cosmetic advice that you can use at home. Look for work attire that makes you feel confident and appealing.

4. Take frequent breaks—schedule time off to unwind to improve your performance. Take a break between jobs to do something enjoyable. Make the most of your vacation time.

5. Maintain your concentration. Focus on completing a single assignment at a time while keeping your professional objectives in mind. Being strategic and aware will enable you to achieve more and improve the quality of your job.

6. Add value to the situation. Consider what you bring to the table at work. Invest your time and resources in the things that will have the most impact.

1. Be generous with your gifts. Give of your time, skills, and hospitality. Look for ways to aid people, whether through actual support or a nice word.

2. Pay attention to what is being said. Give your undivided attention to others. You'll improve your connections and have fewer disputes as a result.

3. Be willing to forgive. Be fast to forgive those who have wronged you. You might repair the relationship, or you could opt to go on. In any case, letting go of any bitterness or injured sentiments will help you.

4. Maintain contact. Take care of the connections that are important to you. Make plans to see friends regularly, and reconnect with old acquaintances you haven't seen in a long time.

5. Share a meal. People get together when they share meals. Have family dinners and arrange potluck events for your friends as often as possible.

6. Make an effort to smile more. Simply putting on a cheerful expression might make you appear more appealing and pleasant. Make a smile-inducing trigger for yourself. It might be a specific word or a common occurrence, such as your phone ringing.

You don't have to move to a new place or train like an Olympic athlete to change your life. Concentrate on only one small activity at a time and watch the rewards accumulate.

20 WAYS TO ENHANCE YOUR
HAPPINESS

Everyone that isn't happy wishes they were. Those that are already happy would like to be even happier. *A life filled with happiness is a worthwhile goal and readily achievable.* A life lacking happiness is a constant challenge. Happiness isn't just about the big things. There are many small items that coloryour life andsubtly add to or subtract from it.

If you'd like to add more happiness to your life, try these tips:

1 Realize that money is great for solving problems, but does littleto increase happiness.

Need new tires on your car? Want to make a career change? Money is a great solution.

However, once you have enough money to meetyour basic needs, happiness is found elsewhere. More money doesn't make you happier.

2 Sleep at least 7 hours each night.

If you think you're thriving on 5 hours of sleep,think again. Every study on the topic has shownthat every measured performance metric improves when sleep is increased to a minimumof 7 hours.

3 Give at least one sincere compliment each day.

Focus on the positive in others. You'll feel betterand receive the same consideration.

4 Be mindful.

Let go of regret and worry. Your life is happening right now. You surely don't want tomiss anything.

5 Eat a healthy breakfast.

Feel good about yourself by getting the day off on the right foot. You'll also be more likely to eat a healthy lunch.

6 Spend regular time on a hobby you love.

Work is required for most of us. Hobbies are optional. Spend part of your free time on activities you do just for fun.

7 Be grateful.

You probably have more good things in your life than you realize. Focus on those good things and your mood is sure to brighten.

8 Get out of the house.

It's easy to get stuck in a rut when you see and experience the same things consistently. See what else is going on in the world.

9 Find middle ground.

Happiness is rarely found at the extremes. The middle path is the sweet spot.

10 Focus on regular improvement instead of perfection.

If being perfect is necessary to feel happy, you're doomed to misery. Be happy with small, consistent improvement.

11 Try something new.

You probably haven't read your favorite book, eaten in your favorite restaurant, or met your favorite person yet.

12 Take a 10-minute break each hour.

Not only will you get more done each day, you'll have more energy at the end of the day to enjoy yourself.

13 Get things done.

Procrastination is a happiness killer. Consider how much stress would be removed from yourlife if you got the essentials done on time.

14 Spend time with those you love.

Few things can enhance your happiness more than spending quality time with those you love.

15 Say "yes."

Some of us are too quick to say "no" to any new opportunity. Make it a point to say yes to new opportunities.

16 Say "no."

Avoid agreeing to new obligations too quickly. If your plate is already full, piling on more responsibilities and commitments will only sour your mood.

17 Smile

Even if you don't feel like it, smile. It's free andyou'll feel just a little happier.

18 Pause

Poor choices can create challenging situations. Before saying something unkind or making a major purchase, take a moment and calm yourself first.

19 Do something you've always wanted to do.

Buy a cat or take piano lessons. Learn to speak French.

20 Introduce yourself to someone new.

The people in your life have a significant impacton your happiness. The person you meet today may become your best friend tomorrow.

Who wouldn't want to experience a greaterlevel of happiness on a regular basis? *It's much easier to behappier than you think.* There are many simple things you can do each dayto enhance your-level of happiness.

7 STEPS TO SOLVE ANY CHALLENGE

It has been stated that life is nothing more than a long series of issues to be addressed that don't stop until you die. The truth isn't nearly bleak, but life isn't without its difficulties. The obstacles you face and the answers you find will differ, but your approach to overcoming them may be consistent.

You can reduce the psychological drama that obstacles might cause if you have a process in place! Try this time-tested method:

1. KEEP A POSITIVE ATTITUDE.

When things don't go as planned, it's all too easy to become down on yourself. Negative thinking, unfortunately, makes you less capable. It can conceal the most definitive answers. Consider problems as puzzles to be solved, expecting that all will work out in the end.

2. CREATE THE PERFECT SOLUTION.

Aiming too low is a bad idea. It's customary to set a goal of just surviving the challenge, but are you capable of going above and beyond? Can you think of a way to improve your circumstances even more than it was before? Make your difficulty a stepping stone to bigger and better things.

3. DISCUSS THE PROBLEM.

A major problem is sometimes the result of a few minor issues. Dealing with one tiny problem at a time will help you develop better control over your capacity to focus and prevent anxiety. You'll gain confidence and momentum as you continue to reduce the scope of the problem.

4. MAINTAIN YOUR FOCUS ON SOLUTIONS.

Don't be concerned about the future. Take your time to come up with the most acceptable option. Look, seek a better answer once you've found a decent one. Continue looking until you're confident you can't find anything better. Keep in mind, too, that you need to give yourself adequate time to respond appropriately.

5. SEEK OUT ASSISTANCE.

Many folks are willing to assist. There's no reason to feel embarrassed about seeking assistance. You'd gladly help a friend or family member. They're also eager to assist you. Do not be afraid to inquire.

6. BE READY FOR THE WORST-CASE SCENARIO.

What could go wrong with your plan? Have cures or preventative measures in place before deciding on a solution to counteract whatever could go wrong.

7. DEVOTE ALL OF YOUR ENERGY TO DEVELOPING YOUR SOLUTION.

Maintain your attention and carry out your strategy. Stay on top of where and how things are changing and make any necessary changes. Unless it's clear that you've picked an unsuccessful approach, never give up.

Use a structured procedure to solve problems and conquer hurdles in life.

Continue to take action until you've found a solution. Maintain an optimistic mindset and be inventive while brainstorming solutions. A challenge may frequently be used to your advantage.

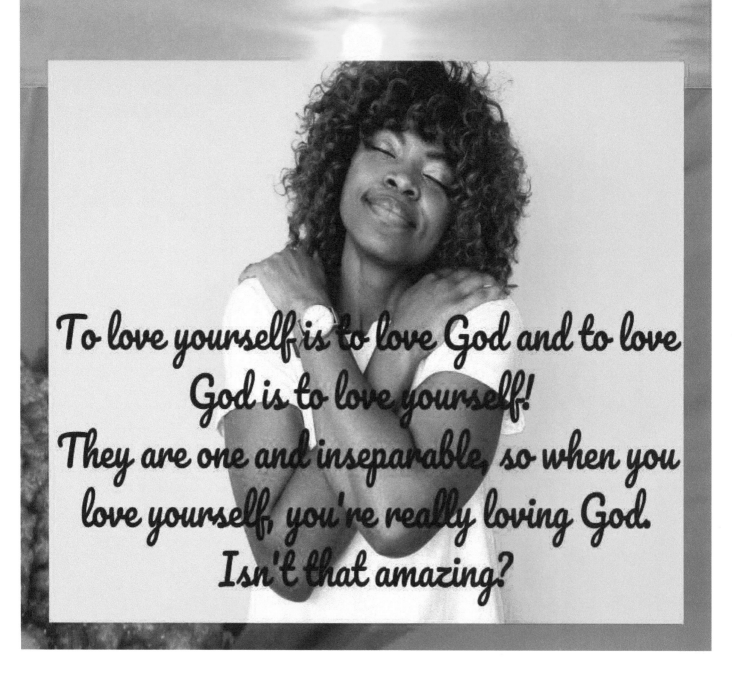

To love yourself is to love God and to love God is to love yourself! They are one and inseparable, so when you love yourself, you're really loving God. Isn't that amazing?

CPSIA information can be obtained
at www.ICGtesting.com
Printed in the USA
LVHW071313301222
736209LV00010B/288